Anonymous

A New Directory for the Public Worship of God

Anonymous

A New Directory for the Public Worship of God

ISBN/EAN: 9783337293260

Printed in Europe, USA, Canada, Australia, Japan

Cover: Foto ©Lupo / pixelio.de

More available books at **www.hansebooks.com**

A NEW DIRECTORY FOR THE PUBLIC WORSHIP OF GOD

A NEW DIRECTORY FOR THE PUBLIC WORSHIP OF GOD

FOUNDED ON THE BOOK OF COMMON ORDER (1560-64) AND THE WESTMINSTER DIRECTORY (1643-45), AND PREPARED BY THE "PUBLIC WORSHIP ASSOCIATION IN CONNECTION WITH THE FREE CHURCH OF SCOTLAND"

"Let all things be done unto edifying."—1 Cor. xiv. 26.
"Let all things be done in seemly form, and according to order."
—1 Cor. xiv. 40.

Edinburgh
MACNIVEN & WALLACE
1898

PREFACE

THE Association by which this Directory for Public Worship has been prepared, was formed at a Conference of Ministers and Elders of the Free Church of Scotland, held at Edinburgh in May 1891. The object of the Association, as stated in its Constitution, is "to promote the ends of edification, order, and reverence in the public services of the Church, in accordance with Scripture principles, and in the light especially of the experience and practice of the Reformed Churches holding the Presbyterian system." The suggestion that such an Association should be formed, and the invitation to the Conference, were contained in a Circular signed by eighteen ministers, namely : — Drs Bannerman, Blaikie, Bruce, A. O. Johnston, Laidlaw, Macmillan, Reith, Ross Taylor, Salmond, Walter C. Smith ; Messrs T. Crerar, Lewis Davidson, J. T. Ferguson, W. A. Gray, T. B. Kilpatrick, D. M. Ross, David Somerville, and George Steven.

In this Circular, those who signed it said they felt that the subject of the Public Worship of the Church called for special consideration at the present time, and that in connection with it there was room and need for improvement in various directions. Their desire was that all efforts for such improvement "should proceed upon lines in harmony with the past history, and best traditions of the Scottish Church in the matter of worship, and should be — to use the language of the Solemn League and Covenant—'in accordance with the Word of God, and the example of the best Reformed Churches,' as represented, for instance, in the General Presbyterian Alliance. In particular, all of us hold strongly that the duty and privilege of *free prayer* in the public Worship of God should be jealously guarded and maintained, and that nothing in the least approaching to a compulsory Liturgy, as in the Anglican and Roman Communions, should be even proposed.

"In the event of union between our own Church and one or both of the other great branches of Presbyterianism in Scotland, which in our opinion is much to be desired, a Revision of the old Scottish Book of Common Order, and of the Westminster Directory for Worship, would probably have to be undertaken by the United Church. In view of such a work in the future, it is of great importance that the mind of the Free Church of Scotland as a whole, and especially of its ministers, should be seriously and prayerfully turned to this question, and that our Church should be in a position to take an intelligent and influential part in the ultimate re-adjustment and improvement of the common standards for worship."

On these lines, the work of the Association has gone forward in a very harmonious and encouraging way for the past seven years. It has sought to call attention, —and has done so, it is believed, with good results —on the one hand, to the danger of hasty and ill-considered action, and of merely imitative movements in the direction of Anglican forms and usages; and on the other hand, to the need of improvements in various respects in the ordinary Public Worship and in the Special Services of the Church, and to the lines on which such improvements may best be carried out, in accordance with Scriptural and confessional principles, and in the light of the practice and experience of sister Reformed Churches both in Great Britain, America, and the Continent of Europe. Papers have been issued yearly for private circulation among the members of the Association; but this "Directory for Worship" is its first publication for general use.

The two well-known Service-books of the Scottish Church, on which this little work is based, may be described respectively as an optional Liturgy and a Directory for Worship.

The Book of Common Order arose out of the form of service drawn up by John Knox, Whittingham, and others for the use of the English exiles at Frankfort in 1554. It was first published at Geneva in 1556, and used in the Church there, in which both Knox and Whittingham were ministers. After Knox's return to Scotland in 1559, "if not earlier, the Book of Geneva began to be used by some of the Reformed Congregations in this country. In the First Book of Discipline, adopted by the Church in 1560, it is said to be 'already used in some of our Churches,' and is spoken of as 'the Book of Our Common Order, called the Order of Geneva.' In 1562 the General Assembly enjoined its uniform use in 'ministration of the Sacraments and solemnisation of marriages and burial of the dead.'[1] It was reprinted in Edinburgh in that year with some additions. Between 1562 and 1564 it was modified and enlarged; new prayers were added from Continental sources, others, which had been used in Scotland previously, were incorporated with it, and the Psalter was completed. In this form it was printed in Edinburgh

[1] *Book of the Universal Kirk*, p. 13. Sess. V. Dec. 31, 1562.

in 1564; and the Assembly of that year 'ordained that every Minister, Exhorter, and Reader shall have one of the Psalm books, lately printed in Edinburgh, and use the Order contained therein in Prayers, Marriage, and Ministration of the Sacraments.'[1]

"The Book of Geneva, thus remodelled, is known as Knox's Liturgy or Book of Common Order; and it embodied the law of the Church as to worship from 1564 to 1645."[2]

The "Book of Common Order," however, is a better and more accurately descriptive name for the first Service-book of the Scottish Reformed Church than "Liturgy," which is apt to suggest a fixed and compulsory form of ritual. In "The Book of Our Common Order," the place and rights of free prayer are carefully vindicated and guarded, an outline of the order of worship is given, with specimen forms of prayer, confession of sins, thanksgiving, and intercession, which, "or such like," the minister is to use. We have an "Order of Baptism," "The Manner of the Administration of the Lord's Supper," "The Form of Marriage," etc., with examples of suitable exhortations, and prayers; and the officiating minister is enjoined to use "either the words following, or like in effect." "The minister exhorting the people to pray, saith in this manner, or such like." "The minister prayeth for the assistance of God's Holy Spirit, as the same shall move His heart, and so proceedeth to the sermon." "After sermon he either

---

[1] Calderwood, *Hist. of the Kirk of Scotland* (Wodrow Soc. ed.), ii. 284.

[2] See Sprott and Leishman's admirable edition of the Book of Common Order and the Westminster Directory, with Historical Introductions and Illustrative Notes. Edin. and London, 1868. Preface, p. xv.

useth the 'Prayer for all Estates,' or else prayeth as the Spirit of God shall move his heart."[1]

It is unnecessary to refer here in detail to the contents of the Westminster Directory, which may be assumed to be in the hands of our ministers generally. We may venture to say, in passing, that it deserves, and will repay, much more careful study on their part than it often receives. It is not indeed of full authority in the Church, and has no direct place in the Ordination vows of her office-bearers; but it contains a great deal that is of very high and permanent value, both in the way of guidance and suggestion in matters of worship. The Westminster Directory traverses, so far, the same ground as the Book of Common Order, but does not give the same amount of help as regards special services. It says nothing whatever, for example, of Ordination Services,—a lack which is somewhat inadequately supplied in the reference to the subject in the other Westminster document known as "The Form of Church Government." As regards the ordinary public worship of the Lord's day, however, the Directory furnishes a considerable amount of valuable material and suggestion for Confession, Adoration, Thanksgiving, Petition, and Intercession, so prepared and arranged that they can, with very little difficulty, be turned into direct forms of prayer.[2]

In the Directory for Public Worship now issued, we follow the Book of Common Order in giving specimen forms for certain parts of the ordinary service, *e.g.*, Prayers of Invocation, of Thanksgiving, and "for all

---

[1] See Dr Jas. Bannerman's account of the Book of Common Order, *Church of Christ*, ii. 414-420.

[2] Compare Sprott and Leishman's *Book of Common Order and Directory*, p. 325.

Estates," giving also somewhat fuller forms for such special services as Baptism, the Lord's Supper, Ordination of Ministers, Elders, and Deacons, Church Dedication, Marriage, and Burial of the Dead. In accordance with the example of the Westminster Directory, a large amount of space has been devoted to materials and suggestions for Confession, Thanksgiving, Petition, and Intercession. It would, of course, have been comparatively easy to provide set forms of prayer under these various heads. To provide and arrange suitable material, which, while not repressing or hampering free prayer, should serve to guide and stimulate it, was a much more difficult task.

The Committee wish to draw special attention to the Confession of Sins, the Prayer of Thanksgiving, the Litany, and the Marriage Service, taken from "Hermann's Consultation."[1] These have been specially translated from the original Latin for this volume. They have not, so far as the Committee are aware, been brought before the Church since the publication of two English editions—both now extremely rare—of the "Pia Deliberatio" in 1547 and 1548.

The very interesting Reformation Service-book, known as "Hermann's Consultation," was prepared by Bucer and Melanchthon at the request of Hermann, the Protestant Elector and Archbishop of Cologne, in the first half of the sixteenth century. It appeared first in German in 1543, then in Latin in 1545, and in English in 1547 and 1548. A fine copy of the Latin edition is preserved in the Advocates' Library, Edinburgh, dated "Bonnae, ex officina Laurentii Mylii Typographi, anno MDXXXXV." The translations in this volume are made from that edition, with comparison of the renderings in the two

[1] See below, pp. 35-38; 73; 94-97; 160-164.

PREFACE.

English editions. One copy of each of these (that of the earlier edition being imperfect) exists in the Bodleian Library at Oxford.[1] Both editions are beautifully printed in black letter. The title of the copy of the first edition, and some pages at beginning and end, are gone.[2] The title of the second edition is as follows :—" A simple and religious Consultation of us Herman by the grace of God, Archbishop of Colone and prince Electoure, &c. by what meanes a Christian Reformation and founded on God's Worde of doctrine administration of devine Sacraments, of Ceremonies and the whole cure of soules and other ecclesiastical ministeries may be begon among men committed to our pastorall charge, until the Lord graunte a better to be appointed, &c. Perused by the translator thereof and amended in many places, 1548. Imprinted at London by Jhon Daye and William Seres, dwellynge in Sepulchres paryshe at the singe of the Resurrection a lytle above Holbourne Conduit."

[1] It is interesting for Scottish readers to remember that this magnificent library is largely due to the munificence of the son of one of John Knox's Elders in the English Church at Geneva. John Bodley, or Bodleigh, was admitted to the Eldership there in 1557. He aided in the translation of the Geneva Bible, and is said to have borne the whole expense of printing it. His eldest son, Thomas, was educated chiefly at Geneva. He was on diplomatic service under Queen Elizabeth, and was knighted by James VI. He endowed and largely increased the University Library at Oxford, hence known, from the name of its chief benefactor, as "the Bodleian." Comp. *Livre des Anglois, or Register of the English Church at Geneva,* 1555-1559—edited by Prof. Mitchell, St Andrews, pp. 5, 9, 12 f.

[2] One perfect copy of the edition of 1547 is preserved, according to the catalogue, in the British Museum Library; but the editor of this work had not an opportunity of consulting it. He desires to acknowledge the great courtesy of the librarians of the Advocates' Library and of the Bodleian, in connection with his references to the copies of the Latin and English editions of Hermann's "Consultation," which are so well cared for by them.

PREFACE

Melanchthon states in one of his letters that the doctrinal part of this Service-book was due to himself, while the prayers and forms of service were prepared by Bucer. He mentions, in particular, that "the Order of Baptism and of the Lord's Supper were composed by him" (Bucer).[1]

The Committee of the Association, on whom the work of preparing this Directory has devolved,[2] are conscious of various defects in what they now submit to the Church, and especially to its ministers. They are the more grateful for the large measure of expressed approval with which several parts of their work have already met, mingled with some kindly and candid criticism from individual members of the Association.

The Committee trust they may be forgiven if they add here a few words of counsel especially to the younger ministers of the Church. We do well to prize and hold fast the freedom which we have in the matter of public prayer, and in the lesser details of the Order of Service. Our Scottish Church since the Reformation has shown practically in this field that she "believes in the Holy Ghost, the Lord, and the Giver of Life," and in His perpetual presence wherever God's people meet for worship in the name of Christ. By her plan of worship, alike under the Book of Common Order and the Westminster Directory, our Church has called upon each of

---

[1] The passage is quoted by Shields, *Liturgia Expurgata* (*The Prayer book as amended by the Westminster Divines*), 4th ed., p. 80.

[2] The names of the Executive Committee to whom this work has been entrusted are :—Rev. Dr Bannerman, Perth (*Convener*); Rev. Prof. Martin, D.D., New Coll., Edinburgh ; Revs. J. T. Ferguson, Cupar-Fife ; J. Henderson, Glasgow ; D. Purves, Gourock ; F. J. Rae, Newport ; D. M. Ross, Glasgow ; R. S. Simpson, Edinburgh ; D. Somerville, Edinburgh (*Secretary*) ; G. Stevens, Edinburgh ; Wm. Cowan, Esq., Edinburgh.

PREFACE. xiii

her ministers to "stir up the gift of God which is in him" for all the work of the ministry, to which he was solemnly set apart by prayer, "with the laying on of the hands of the Presbytery." She shows that she expects him not only to preach the Gospel, but to cultivate the power of leading the devotions of a congregation in such a way as really to meet and give expression to the spiritual wants and cravings of the earnest and living members of the Church. He is thereby shut up, in a most wholesome way, by the very necessities of the case, to "take heed to himself" and his own spiritual life, and to cast himself very specially on the promise and help of the Holy Spirit. The result has been, with all our defects, a decidedly high average of attainment among the ministers of the Scottish Church, not only in preaching—but in the gift of edifying and acceptable public prayer.

But this liberty ought not to become license—as there is sometimes a tendency for it to do—in the hands of any of our ministers. It was always meant by the Church to be "freedom in the bounds of law,"—"the law of the Spirit of life in Christ Jesus," the law which bids us "consider one another in love," and "look not to our own things merely, but the things of others." In the order and manner of public worship, the general historical usages of the Scottish Church ought not to be rashly and needlessly departed from. Even the local traditions and customs of a congregation or district ought to be duly considered, and no hasty changes made, however reasonable in themselves these may appear to a young minister.

Above all, every minister should beware of obtruding his own personal moods and experiences upon the people in prayer, of varying the accustomed Order of

PREFACE.

Service without special and intelligible reasons, of partial and capricious choice of topics in prayer. Ministers ought, in short, to realise their high position and responsibility as the leaders of public worship, and seek by suitable preparation to fulfil the functions of their position intelligently and sympathetically. In the Westminster Directory, which, under English Puritan influences as to worship, went further in the direction of freedom than the earlier Service-book of the Scottish Church, the importance of general uniformity of order, and of meeting the stated spiritual necessities of the congregation in the prayers of the ordinary Lord's Day Service, were distinctly recognised and provided for. "Our meaning is," the Westminster Divines say in their Directory, "that the general heads, the sense and scope of the prayers, and other parts of public worship being known to all, there may be a consent of all the Churches in those things that contain the substance of the Service and Worship of God; and the ministers may be hereby directed, in their administrations, to keep like soundness in doctrine and prayer, and may, if need be, have some help and furniture; and yet so as they become not hereby slothful or negligent in stirring up the gifts of Christ in them; but that each one, by meditation, by taking heed to himself and the flock of God committed to him, and by wise observing the ways of Divine Providence, may be careful to furnish his heart and tongue with further or other materials of prayer and exhortation, as shall be needful upon all occasions."

In name of the Committee,
D. DOUGLAS BANNERMAN,
*President of the Public Worship Association
in connection with the Free Church of Scotland.*

EDINBURGH, *April*, 1898.

CONTENTS.

PART I.

ORDINARY PUBLIC WORSHIP OF THE LORD'S DAY: WITH NOTES ON CERTAIN PARTS OF IT.

	PAGES
ORDER OF SERVICE AT ORDINARY DIET OF WORSHIP .	1-3
SECTION I. Prayer of Invocation . .	4-13
,, II. Confession of Sins . . .	13-38
,, III. Petition	38-59
,, IV. Thanksgiving	59-74
,, V. Intercession . . .	74-97
,, VI. Prayer for Illumination, or for the Holy Spirit	97-100

PART II.

THE SACRAMENTS.

SECTION I. Baptism—(A) Baptism of Infants . .	101-118
(B) Baptism of Adults .	118-124
,, II. The Lord's Supper, or the Communion .	124-145

CONTENTS.

PART III.

ORDER OF SERVICES ON SPECIAL OCCASIONS.

PAGES

SECTION I. Admission of Baptized Persons to the full Communion of the Church — Young Communicants 147-154

,, II. Marriage 154-164

,, III. Burial of the Dead 165-185

,, IV. Ordination and Induction of a Minister . 185-205

,, V. Ordination and Admission of Elders and Deacons 205-219

,, VI. Licensing of Probationers . . . 219-225

,, VII. Dedication of a Church . . . 226-238

Directory for the Public Worship of God:

Founded on the Book of Common Order (1560-64), *and the Westminster Directory* (1643-45), *and prepared by the " Public Worship Association in connection with the Free Church of Scotland."*

Part I.

ORDINARY PUBLIC WORSHIP OF THE LORD'S DAY.

ORDER OF SERVICE AT AN ORDINARY DIET OF WORSHIP.

	1.	One or more Sentences of Scripture.
I.	2.	Prayer of Invocation (brief).
II.	3.	Praise—Psalm or Hymn.
III.	4.	First Reading of Scripture (O.T.), *or* after (5)—*i.e.* 4 and 5 transposed.
IV.	5.	Prayer of—Adoration, Thanksgiving and Confession; for pardon and cleansing; for grace and every blessing.
	6.	Praise—Psalm sung or chanted, Hymn or Anthem.
V.	7.	Second Reading of Scripture (N.T.).
	8.	Praise.
VI.	9.	Prayer of Intercession, ending with Lord's Prayer.

A

VII. 10. Praise.
      11. Prayer for Illumination (brief).
VIII. 12. Sermon or Lecture.
      13. Praise.
IX.   14. Prayer for blessing on the preaching of the Word, for Guidance and Protection.
X.   15. Praise—Doxology.
XI.   16. Benediction.

NOTE.—(1) Words to children may follow either Reading of Scripture or may be founded on a children's text and hymn after 9.
    (2) Intimations either before 10 or before 15.
    (3) Collection or offertory may be taken during 10 or 15. The English Presbyterian Directory puts it before 15.
    (4) Those portions of the above order not found in the first column of figures are to be regarded as less essential than the rest.

ORDER OF SERVICE RECOMMENDED

IN

I.—The Book of Common Order :—
1. Prayer of Invocation.
2. Reading of Old Testament Scriptures. } Reader's
3. Reading of New Testament Scriptures. } Service.
4. Psalm.
5. Prayer of Confession : for pardon, cleansing and grace.
6. Psalm.
7. Prayer, especially for the Holy Spirit.
8. Sermon or Lecture.

9. Prayer for the whole estate of Christ's Church, for nations and rulers, &c.
10. Lord's Prayer.
11. Repetition of Apostles' Creed.
12. Psalm.
13. Benediction.

II.—The Westminster Directory for Public Worship:—
1. Prayer of Invocation.
2. Reading of Old Testament Scriptures.
3. Reading of New Testament Scriptures.
4. Exposition, "if judged necessary, after the Chapter or Psalm be ended . . . regard being had always unto the time . . . which rule is to be observed in all other public performances."
5. Psalm.
6. Prayer of Confession: for pardon and cleansing; for the Holy Spirit; [Thanksgivings; Special Petitions and Intercessions]; for blessing on the Word to be preached.*
7. Sermon or Lecture.
8. Prayer: Thanksgivings; [Intercessions and Special Petitions]; for blessing on the preaching of the Word.
9. Lord's Prayer.
10. Psalm.
11. Benediction.

* The parts included in brackets in 6 and 8 may be transposed, "as the minister shall think meet."

ORDINARY SERVICE OF LORD'S DAY, WITH NOTES ON CERTAIN PARTS OF IT.

SECTION I.

PRAYER OF INVOCATION.

"THE Congregation being assembled, the Minister, after solemn calling on them to the worshipping of the great Name of God, is to begin with prayer."—(Westminster Directory for Public Worship.)

The call to worship may be conveyed in the simplest form: "Let us worship God," "Let us pray," or in an Introductory Sentence or Sentences of Scripture, followed by a brief Prayer of Invocation, such as those now given :—

1

How excellent is Thy lovingkindness, O God; therefore do the children of men put their trust under the shadow of Thy wings. Satisfy us now with the goodness of Thy House. In Thy light make us to see light. May Thy Holy Spirit be with us in prayer and praise, in speaking and hearing from Thy Holy Word. And do Thou bless us with all spiritual blessing in Jesus Christ, for His name's sake. Amen.

2

O God, the preparation of the heart and the opening of the lips are from Thee. Quicken us after Thy lovingkindness, that we may call aright upon Thy name. Meet with us in prayer and praise and in the Word. Make this a day of grace and blessing to us all in Thy House, for Jesus' sake. Amen.

3

Almighty and everlasting God, teach us to worship Thee who art a Spirit in spirit and in truth. Take away all blindness of heart, all coldness and backwardness of spirit. Open Thou our lips, and our mouth shall show forth Thy praise. Open our hearts to receive Thy truth in the love of it. May Christ be glorified in the preaching of His Gospel, and in all the services of His House this day, for His name's sake. Amen.

4

O God, the Father of Mercies and the God of all grace, let all those who seek Thee in this Thy House to-day rejoice and be glad in Thee. If there are some here who feel that they are poor and needy, make them to know that Thou the Lord thinkest on them. Be their Help and Deliverer now. Prepare our hearts for praise and prayer, and for Thy Holy Word. And bless us all, above our askings, for Jesus' sake. Amen.

Here follow Scriptures which may be made use of in Prayers of Invocation :—

Who shall ascend into the hill of the Lord?
   or who shall stand in His holy place?
      He that hath clean hands and a pure heart
      who hath not lifted up his soul unto vanity
      nor sworn deceitfully.
      Cleanse us from all our iniquities
      and cause us to dwell in Thy presence.

The eyes of all things wait upon Thee
     and Thou givest them their meat in due season
     Thou openest Thy hand,
        and satisfiest the desire of every living thing.

The Lord is nigh unto all them that call upon Him,
to all that call upon Him in truth.
Ps. cxlv. The Lord preserveth all them that love Him.

God is our king of old, working salvation in the midst of the earth.
The day is Thine, the night also is Thine:
Thou hast prepared the light and the sun:
Thou hast set all the borders of the earth:
Thou hast made summer and winter.
O forget not the life of Thy poor for ever,
Ps. lxxiv. let the poor and needy praise Thy name.

Bow down Thine ear, O Lord, and hear us,
for we are poor and needy.
Preserve our souls, for we are Thy children
O Thou our God, save Thy servants that trust in Thee,
Rejoice our souls, for unto Thee do we lift them up,
for Thou, Lord, art good, and ready to forgive
and plenteous in mercy unto all them that call
Ps. lxxxvi. upon Thee.

Thou hast ascended on high:
Thou hast led Thy captivity captive
Thou hast received gifts among men,
yea, among the rebellious also
that the Lord God might dwell with them.
Blessed be the Lord, who daily beareth our burden
Ps. lxviii. even the God who is our salvation.

It is a good thing to give thanks unto the Lord
and to sing praises unto Thy name, O most High
to show forth Thy lovingkindness in the morning
and Thy faithfulness every night.

SEC. I.]   *PRAYER OF INVOCATION.*

For Thou, Lord, hast made us glad thro' Thy work
   we will triumph in the works of Thy hands.
      How great are Thy works, O Lord :
Ps. xcii. Thy thoughts are very deep.

O Lord, open Thou our lips
   and our mouth shall show forth Thy praise.
   For Thou desirest not sacrifice, else would we give it
      Thou delightest not in burnt offering
   the sacrifices of God are a broken spirit ;
      a broken and a contrite heart, O God, Thou wilt
Ps. li.   not despise.

This is the day which the Lord hath made,
   we will rejoice and be glad in it.
   This is the gate of the Lord :
      the righteous shall enter into it.
   Open unto us the gates of righteousness,
      we will enter into them
Ps. cxviii. and will give thanks unto Thee, O Lord.

The Lord is a great God
   and a great king above all gods.
   In His hand are the deep places of the earth :
      the heights of the mountains are His also.
      the sea is His, and He made it
      and His hands formed the dry land.
         O come, let us worship and bow down
         let us kneel before the Lord our Maker
         For He is our God,
Ps. xcv.   and we are the people of His pasture.

The Lord is our light and our salvation: whom shall we fear?
the Lord is the strength of our life: of whom shall we be afraid?
   Though an host should encamp against us,
      our heart shall not fear:
   though war should rise against us,
      even then will we be confident.
        Hide not Thy face from us:
        Thou hast been our help, leave us not,
           neither forsake us, O God of our
Ps. xxvii. 1, 3, 9.   salvation.

The Lord is in His holy temple:
the Lord's throne is in heaven:
His eyes behold, His eyelids try the children of men,
He trieth the righteous.
   O God, try us and know our thoughts
   and see if there be any wicked way in us,
   and lead us in the way everlasting.
Ps. xi. 139.

Lord, who shall abide in Thy tabernacle?
   who shall dwell in Thy holy hill?
He that walketh uprightly and worketh righteousness and speaketh the truth in his heart.
   Create in us a clean heart, O God,
   and renew a right spirit within us.

As the hart panteth after the water-brooks
   so panteth our soul after Thee, O God.
      O send out Thy light and Thy truth, let them lead us
     let them bring us unto Thy holy hill
        and to Thy tabernacles.

PRAYER OF INVOCATION.

    Then will we go unto the altar of God
        unto God our exceeding joy
       and upon the harp will we praise Thee,
Ps. xlii., xliii.   O God our God.

God is our refuge and strength, a very present help in trouble,
    Therefore will we not fear, tho' the earth be removed
    and tho' the mountains be carried into the midst of the sea,
      For Thou, O Lord of hosts, art with us,
Ps. xlvi.   Thou, O God of Jacob, art our refuge.

How amiable are Thy tabernacles, O Lord of Hosts:
    Our soul longeth, yea, even fainteth for the courts of the Lord,
    Our heart and our flesh cry out for the living God.
      Blessed are they that dwell in Thy house,
        they will be still praising Thee.
      Blessed is the man whose strength is in Thee,
Ps. lxxxiv.   in whose hearts are the highways to Zion.

  O Lord God of Hosts, hear our prayer: give ear, O God of Jacob,
    A day in Thy courts is better than a thousand,
      We had rather stand at the threshold of Thy house
        than dwell in the tents of wickedness.
        O Lord, be our sun and shield;
          give us grace and glory.
           Withhold no good thing from us.
        O Lord of Hosts, bless us who trust in
Ps. lxxxiv.   Thee.

Thy mercy, O Lord, is in the heavens :
> Thy faithfulness reacheth unto the clouds
> Thy righteousness is like the great mountains
> Thy judgments are a great deep.
How excellent is Thy lovingkindness, O God,
> [therefore we] the children of men take refuge
Ps. xxxvi.   under the shadow of Thy wings.

How excellent is Thy lovingkindness, O God,
> therefore the children of men take refuge
> under the shadow of Thy wings.
> They shall be abundantly satisfied with the
> > fatness of Thy house
> and Thou shalt make them drink of the river of
> > Thy pleasures.
> For with Thee is the fountain of life :
> in Thy light shall we see light.
O continue Thy lovingkindness to them that know Thee
> and Thy righteousness to the upright in heart.
Ps. xxxvi.

O God, Thou art our God, early will we seek Thee,
our soul thirsteth for Thee, our flesh longeth for Thee
> in a dry and weary land, where no water is.
Because Thy lovingkindness is better than life
> our lips shall praise Thee :
> so will we bless Thee while we live :
> we will lift up our hands in Thy name.
Ps. lxiii.

Praise waiteth for Thee, O God, in Zion :
> and unto Thee shall the vow be performed.
> O Thou that hearest prayer, unto Thee shall
> > all flesh come.

SEC. I.] *PRAYER OF INVOCATION.* 11

Blessed is the man whom Thou choosest
    and causest to approach unto Thee,
    that he may dwell in Thy courts.
    O, satisfy us with the goodness of Thy house,
Ps. lxv.   even of Thy holy temple.

O Lord, when our spirit is overwhelmed within us
    then Thou knowest our path :
  when refuge fails us, and no man cares for our soul
    then Thou art our refuge, our portion
        in the land of the living,
        attend unto our cry, O Lord, and deliver us.
        Bring our souls out of prison
Ps. cxlii.   that we may give thanks unto Thy name.

Lord, we stretch forth our hands unto Thee,
    our soul thirsteth after Thee, as a weary land.
    Cause us to hear Thy lovingkindness in
        the morning,
        for in Thee do we trust.
    Cause us to know the way wherein we should walk,
Ps. cxliii.   for we lift up our soul unto Thee.

Great is the Lord, and greatly to be praised ;
    His greatness is unsearchable.
    One generation shall praise Thy works to another,
        and shall declare Thy mighty works.
        We will speak of the glorious honour of Thy
            majesty
Ps. cxlv.   and of Thy mighty works.

They that trust in the Lord are as Mount Zion
    which cannot be moved, but abideth for ever.
  As the mountains are round about Jerusalem
    so the Lord is round about His people
      from this time forth and for evermore.
        Do good, O Lord, unto those that be good
          and to them that are upright in their hearts.

Ps. cxxv.

We wait for the Lord, our soul doth wait,
    and in His word do we hope.
  Our soul waiteth for the Lord
    more than they that watch for the morning
    yea, more than they that watch for the morning.
      O Lord, we hope in Thee
        for with Thee there is mercy
        and with Thee there is plenteous redemption.
      And Thou shalt redeem us from all our iniquities.

Ps. cxxx.

Behold, the eye of the Lord is upon them that fear Him,
    upon them that hope in His mercy,
  to deliver their soul from death
  and to keep them alive in famine.
      Our souls wait for Thee, O Lord;
        be Thou our help and our shield.
      Let Thy mercy, O Lord, be upon us
      according as we hope in Thee.

Ps. xxxiii.

We will bless the Lord at all times;
  His praise shall continually be in our mouth.
  Our souls shall make their boast in the Lord.

O magnify the Lord, and let us exalt His name together
   who hath delivered us from all our fears
   and saved us out of all our troubles.
Ps. xxxiv.

The eyes of the Lord are upon the righteous,
   and His ears are open unto their cry.
   They cry, and the Lord heareth
      and delivereth them out of all their troubles.
   The Lord is nigh unto them that are of a broken heart
      and saveth such as be of a contrite spirit.
   The Lord redeemeth the soul of His servants
      and none of them that trust in Him shall be
Ps. xxxiv.   desolate.

SECTION II.

CONFESSION OF SINS.

Although the materials and suggestions for Confession in the following pages are almost entirely for the confession of special sins, this is not because sin itself is thought to be a less important subject of confession either in public or private prayer. On the contrary, it rightly holds a foremost place in those two noble "Confessions of Sin," from the Reformation period, which are given in the Appendix. But the sense of sin comes to most men through the commission of particular sins, or the omission of particular duties. The leading forms of sin and shortcoming are, therefore, here specified, in order that the minister may touch every conscience in turn, and awaken in every heart the sense of sin, and the desire to confess and to forsake it, and to receive forgiveness, cleansing, and renewal.

As will be seen at once, the Ten Commandments have guided the general arrangement; and the subdivisions have been taken from the very full and suggestive exposition of the Commandments in the Larger Catechism. Details have been gathered from the works of the best devotional writers, especially Bishop Andrews, and Bishop Jeremy Taylor.

TITLES OF INVOCATION IN CONFESSION.

1. O Lord, O Lord God, merciful and gracious, long-suffering and abundant in goodness and truth.

2. Keeping mercy for thousands, forgiving iniquity and transgression and sin.

3. Who art a God, ready to pardon, gracious and merciful, slow to anger and of great kindness.

4. Who art a refuge for the oppressed, a refuge in time of trouble, who will never forsake them that seek Thee.

5. Who art nigh unto them that are of a broken heart, and savest such as be of a contrite spirit.

6. Whose mercy is in the heavens, and Thy faithfulness reacheth unto the clouds.

7. Who art rich in mercy.

8. Who will not always chide, neither wilt Thou keep Thine anger for ever.

9. Who dost not deal with us after our sins nor rewardest us according to our iniquities.

10. Whose mercy is from everlasting to everlasting upon them that fear Thee.

11. Who hast made known the exceeding riches of Thy grace.

12. Who art good to all, and Thy tender mercies are over all Thy works.

13. Who is a God like unto Thee that pardonest iniquity and passest by the transgression of the remnant of Thy heritage.

14. Who will turn again and have compassion upon us.

15. Subduing our iniquities and casting all our sins into the depth of the sea.

PLEADINGS.

1. Plead the mercy of God.
    His readiness to forgive.
    His invitation to sinners.
        that we are his children:
        that we are more to Him than the birds of the air or the flowers of the field:
        that He has no pleasure in the death of the wicked.
2. Plead the promises of God.
    that we shall not seek His face in vain:
    that He is faithful and just to forgive.
3. Plead the merits of Christ.
    that our salvation was His purpose:
        by His birth, temptations, trials:
        by His agony, crucifixion, resurrection.
4. Plead our own frailties.
    What is man. . . .
        as the flowers of the field, as grass, shadow.
    The weakness of our flesh, nature, will.
    Our sense of guilt, unworthiness.

5. Plead the power and dominion of sin.
   Our captivity.
   Our corruption—in imagination, affections.
   Subtlety of sin.
   Strength of temptation.

Scripture Pleadings.

1. Blot out our transgressions as a cloud.
2. Remember, O Lord, Thy tender mercies, and Thy loving-kindness, for they have been ever of old.
3. For Thy name's sake, O Lord, pardon our iniquity, for it is great.
4. Have mercy upon us, O God, according to Thy loving-kindness, according to the multitude of Thy tender mercies blot out our transgressions.
5. Wash us throughly from our iniquity and cleanse us from our sin.
6. Purge us with hyssop and we shall be clean, wash us and we shall be whiter than snow.
7. Hide Thy face from our sins and blot out all our iniquities.
8. O remember not against us our former iniquities.
9. Let Thy tender mercies speedily prevent us.
10. Help us, O God of our salvation, for the glory of Thy name.
11. Heal our backslidings, and love us freely.
&c., &c.

Forms.

For . . .
For all our } Have mercy upon us.
For the sins of

CONFESSION OF SINS.

We confess that } But we repent :
We mourn over } Spare us :
We lament   } We plead for mercy,

O God, Who art,
    Who hast,   } Have mercy upon us.

I.—Confession of Sins against God.

1. Our ignorance of God.
    We have not desired Thee or cared to know Thee :
    nor sought for Thee as for hid treasure :
    nor meditated on Thy truth.

2. Our unfaithfulness to God and His truth.
    We have not acknowledged Thee to be our God
    not worshipped Thee in sincerity and truth :
    not submitted to Thy will ;
    not followed in Thy way.
    We have said we knew Thee, and yet denied Thee in our deeds :
    had unworthy thoughts of Thy ways :
    had rebellious thoughts of Thy dealings with us.

3. Our living without God.
    We have forgotten Thee in the hour of prosperity :
    not trusted Thee in danger, want :
    not brought our burdens and fears to Thee :
    marred our lives with anxiety, as if we had no Father in heaven,
    with needless fears, as if all things did not work for good to those who loved Thee :
    trusted more in man's help than in Thine :
    more in wealth than in righteousness :

B

in talent than in holy living:
in anger than in meekness.
Sometimes when we obeyed Thy law, we in heart disliked it.
We have never fully trusted to overcome evil with good, or been able to accept wrong and injury and mockery in patience.
We have believed more in self-assertion than in self-sacrifice,
more in boasting than in humility.
We have loved our own way more than Thine;
our own opinion more than the peace of Thy people.
We have sought the glory of our own name, even when we said we were seeking Thine.

4. Our want of love.
We are too easily turned from Thee by mockery or fear of earthly loss:
too easily turned aside by hopes of gain or praise.
We have little time for Thee because we are so busy with the world.
We find it hard to love one another, but hardest of all to love Thee.
We care more for the friendship of Thine enemies than the friendship of thy Son.
We find time for converse with any one but Thee; to read any book but thine.

5. Our want of zeal for God and his Kingdom.
We do little for Christ's cause and yet are content.

We have little sorrow over our meanness:
worldliness;
little interest in the saving of the world.
We are seldom grieved by the thought of others' sins.
We do little for the heathen abroad or at our doors.
We have wronged good causes by our indifference, suspicions,
and by our cold and critical words.
Even when our zeal in Thy cause is kindled,
we are unwise, rash, self-willed, blind:
use unlawful means to accomplish Thy purpose:
trust in worldly methods more than in gentleness, mercy, long-suffering, &c.

6. Our want of joy in God's service.
Thy service has often been a weariness.
We have been slow to enter on it, ready to be done.
We have felt it a relief when prayer was ended, that we might return to work, play, book.
Glad when godly conversation ceased.

7. Our unthankfulness for God's mercies.
We have neglected Thee in times of joy, success,
and murmured against Thee in times of distress, trial.
When we failed we complained of Thee,
and when we succeeded we took the credit to ourselves.
We ascribed Thy good gifts to our own efforts, skill,

Even when we thanked Thee we have been grudging in our thanks.

Thy good gifts lead us not to repentance, but to pride, vanity, boasting.

8. Our impatience.

We can hardly trust Thee where we must trust Thee alone—where there are no signs of success.

We have fretted under little trials, crosses, and worries.

We are impatient under the cares of home,
the difficulties of daily work, discipline of daily life.

We cannot believe that the Cross is the way of Victory,
that trials are our opportunity of conquering our hearts.

We can scarcely forgive once.

We do not try to forgive others as we ask Thee to forgive us, every morning and every evening.

[Our impatience in time of sickness, pain, sorrow, great loss.]

9. Insincere worship.

We have served Thee that we might be seen of men :
served Thee, but not in spirit and truth :
with our lips, when heart was far away :
in word, while our heart was with the world :
with that which cost us nothing, the sick, torn, lame.

We have found Thy service a weariness, because our hearts were far from Thee.

We are not always thinking of Thee, the living God, in our songs of praise.

A trifle detains us from thy worship,

We are easily distracted in it.

10. Sins in Prayer.

We pray too often that we may persuade Thee to *our* way, desire; and not that we attain to Thy holy and loving will.

We desire not to will that which we hear from Thee, so much as to hear from thee that which we will.

We have often neglected to pray at all.

We omit it on a trivial pretext—because of our work, fatigue, even Christian duties.

We acknowledge our want of thought during prayer, want of attention, reverence.

We confess sin, yet without sorrow or shame.

We confess sin and then turn to it again.

We ask forgiveness, and refuse to forgive others.

We wrestle in prayer only when we are seeking earthly blessings or fearing earthly loss.

We pray because we are afraid not to pray.

We pray, and yet live as if we never expected an answer.

11. Sins in connection with God's Word and His House.

We neglect Thy Word—the Bibles of some unopened since last Sabbath.

We too often come to Church without a thought of meeting Thee :

not hungering after righteousness :

not caring to be humbler, meeker, holier:
not even desiring a better life.
We have sometimes come not to worship Thee, or be taught of Thee, or be strengthened to obey Thee; but merely to be pleased or interested, or from custom.
We come with our minds full of business.
We have been tempted to change Thy Word into a jest.
We have forgot Thee as soon as the hour of service was over.
We do not use the power of Thy fellowship in Church for the work of the Week.

12. Irreverence.
We do not always speak of thee with godly fear.
We do not think of Thee as the Almighty God,
as the awful and righteous Judge,
as the Father of the Holy Jesus Christ.
We have often spoken lightly of things divine:
of things noble, pure, worthy, of good report:
of persons humble, gentle, brave, patient:
of persons deformed by Thy Act, afflicted through no sin of theirs, marred by Thy hand.

13. Sins in connection with Vows and Resolutions.
We have made vows that were unworthy, un-Christian.
We have broken vows that were good.
We have pledged ourselves in frivolous mood.
We have taken oaths that were unlawful, and so have sinned:
we have fulfilled them, and have sinned the more.

14. Blasphemy.
>We have mocked Thy ways in the lives of other men :
>>scorned Thy methods when they were hard :
>>reviled Thy people for deeds that were God-like, for their patience, meekness, self-sacrifice :
>>opposed Thy way when taken by those we disliked, hated, were jealous of.

II.—CONFESSION OF SINS AGAINST OUR FELLOWMEN.

1. We have not regarded a brother's dignity, worth, interests :
>nor honoured or esteemed him better than ourselves :
>nor rejoiced in his gifts, advancement.

    We have tried to undervalue him :
>envied his success, talents, attainments :
>grieved at his prosperity :
>resented his outstripping us in life :
>sacrificed his happiness to our own ends.

2. To superiors.
>We have been undutiful, disobedient to those over us.
>We mourn over our slothfulness, unfaithfulness, as servants.
>We are slow to begin our work, eager to have done.
>How easy for us all to be rude and grudging in our service.
>How hard to be patient, unmurmuring :
>>to be gentle to masters who wrong us :

to be good to masters who are evil.
When reviled, we answer again.
We have flattered our superiors to serve our own ends, and then we have disdained them.

3. To inferiors.
We have sometimes been careless to cruelty towards the poor.
Because they were poor, we forgot they were Thy children, and heirs of Thy Kingdom.

4. We have sometimes commanded things that were unjust, untrue, unseemly.
We have encouraged and favoured what was evil:
discouraged what was good and worthy:
left our neighbour exposed to wrong, temptation.

5. Duties to parents, children, &c.

6. God of all gentleness, have mercy upon us, for being angry without a cause:
our desire of revenge, when vengeance is Thine:
our hatred against any child of Thine:
our speaking words that provoked to anger:
our prejudices against a brother:
our harbouring secret grudges against another:
our being implacable towards an enemy:
our spirit of strife, quarrelling, contention:
anything we have said or done that has broken the peace of our home, our congregation.

7. O God, who art full of tenderness and sympathy and mercy, forgive our unforgiving words:

our unkindly, unfeeling, unsympathetic conversation:
our silence when others were unkind, cruel:
our own cruel words—resentful, revengeful:
our wounding souls through scandal:
our hurting a brother's feelings:
our words that were meant to cut and rankle.

8. O Father, whose thoughts towards us are love, forgive our want of thought for one another:
our hardness of heart:
our shutting up our compassion for the needy:
our indifference to them, ignorance of them:
our quenching thoughts of kindliness, forgiveness:
our want of quietness of mind:
our uncharitable judgments of men:
that we are not gentle and courteous in speech even to those who insult us:
our want of forbearance to the ignorant, the slow, the wilful:
that we are not ready to be reconciled to those who have wronged us or whom we have wronged.

9. O Lord, Who art of purer eyes than to behold evil, we mourn over all our impurity of life and thought:
over all impurity in affections, imagination, words, or behaviour:
our want of watchfulness over thought, heart, conduct:
all unseemliness in speech and behaviour.
We lament that we have listened to corrupt com-

munications when we should have rebuked them: everything we have done that suggested evil to others: idleness that ministers to thoughts of evil.

As a nation we mourn and lament over foolish jesting and talk that is unbecoming, over those men and women made in Thine image who live to debase and destroy their fellows.

10. O Lord, who alone art faithful and true,
we confess all our unfaithfulness.
Thou knowest what wrongs are done among us :
what unfairness in contracts :
what dishonesty in business :
what oppression of the poor, what extortion :
what bribery, what covetousness.
We think too much of gain and too little of men's souls.
Men add field to field and drive Thy people from the land:
make haste to be rich at the cost of a brother:
grow rich and despise Thee.
We mourn over our nation's luxurious living, prodigality, wastefulness.

11. Idleness.
Almighty God, who art ever working for our good,
we mourn over any neglect of work of which we have been guilty :
our want of diligence in it :
our want of care in what thou bestowest :

our distracting care about the future, what we shall eat and drink, and wherewithal shall we be clothed.

12. Our love of money.
O Lord, who possessest all things and madest thyself poor for men,
we mourn over our trust in money rather than in Thy loving protection:
over our too eager desire to get it:
our discontent without it.
Men keep it as if Thou hadst not made them stewards:
seek it as if it would never perish.
We have not given it freely even for the preaching of Thy Gospel.
We have spent lavishly on our own desires and grudged Thy Church a little.

13. O God, who art light and truth, and with Whom is no darkness,
we mourn over our love of that which is not true:
that we have too often prejudiced or perverted the truth:
if we have hurt the good name of others:
if we have sometimes supported an evil cause and have withstood and overborne a good.

14. We have called evil good, and good evil:
sometimes praised, rewarded wickedness, excused or extenuated sin, censured righteousness.
We have been silent when we should have defended the right or withstood the wrong:

or when we spoke, we spoke unreasonably, maliciously, or with a wrong intention.

15. O God, have mercy upon us if at any moment we have been guilty of slandering a brother:
back-biting, detracting:
tale-bearing, scoffing, reviling:
misconstruing his words, actions, intentions:
flattering him.

16. Have mercy upon us if we have at any time spread a false report:
endeavoured or desired to impair the credit of others:
rejoiced in their disgrace, loss, failure:
suspected evil of those who were good:
spoken against or felt contempt for any child of Thine:
neglected to speak well of those who were wrongly reviled,
or to hide the shame of a brother,
or to defend the innocent.
We mourn that we are so ready to believe evil of men, so slow to believe good.
We mourn that it is hard to study and practise those things that are true, noble, just, pure, lovely, of good report, virtuous, praiseworthy.

17. Have mercy upon us, for we are often discontented with our condition,
with Thy dealings, discipline, chastisement:
envying and grieving at the good of others:
vexed that others are better than we, that they are placed in more favourable circum-

stances, born with fewer temptations in body and soul:
uncharitable and unkindly in thought towards others:
unwilling to further another's cause.

III.—Confession of Sins against the Gospel and the Holy Spirit.

1. O God, who hast commanded the light to shine out of darkness,
we confess and lament that we have loved the darkness rather than the light:
that we have turned away from the knowledge of the Son of God:
that we have let sin gain dominion over us:
not walked in the Spirit:
not cared to be saved from ourselves:
followed the judgments of men:
feared their blame and not Thine:
neglected Thy grace in our temptations:
not trusted Thy strength in our weakness.

2. Almighty Father, who hast so loved us that Thou gavest Thy Son to death for us,
we mourn that His death has awakened so little love in our hearts for Thee:
so little gratitude to Him:
that our sins do not alway bring us to His cross.
We have little desire to be wholly consecrated to His service:
to live humbly working for Thee.
We can hardly work for Christ without worldly recognition.

3. O Heavenly Father, we mourn over our earthliness of heart :
that we seek our own success even in Thy work :
we care too much for pleasure, and too little for Christ :
we fear punishment more than offending Him :
when burdened and distressed, we do not come at once to Him for refuge and rest :
we have been ashamed to confess Him, because of the mocking of men :
when His cause was unpopular :
when it meant earthly loss :
that the love of Christ does not constrain us,
that our hearts are cold towards Him,
our hearts are so slow to trust Him.

4. O God, who hast sent Thy Spirit to bear witness in our hearts to the truth and love of Thy Son, and to work in us Thy Holy will, we lament that we have not profited, as we ought to have done, by His gracious ministry :
that we have, by our carnal and worldly desires, crushed the good impulses, and turned aside from the vision of a heavenly life, that have come from Thine inspiration :
that we have not exercised the gifts of Thy Spirit, or made use of the powers of usefulness in the service of our fellow-men Thou hast bestowed :
that we have often resisted the gracious workings of Thy Spirit, that we have hardened our hearts against the good example of Thy servants, and been deaf to their words of entreaty :

that we have grieved Thy Spirit by our coldness,
by our unwillingness to repent and believe in
Thy Son, by our wilful opposition to Thy
truth :

that we have often quenched Thy Spirit within us,
preferring the traditions of men, and the customs
of the world to the truth and holiness of Thy
Gospel,

holding by the forms of past thought when Thou
wouldst have led us unto a further knowledge
of Thy ways :

that we have not walked in Thy Spirit but have
often trusted to our own wisdom :

have been guided by worldly expediency and
the counsels of the flesh :

that we have indulged the appetite of the body
in opposition to holy impulse.

5. O Lord, who hast in Thy great mercy given us a
day of rest in which to meet Thee,
we mourn that we have often neglected it :
have not made it a time of fellowship with
Thee :
a day for thought and reverence :
an opportunity of rising into Thy pure life :
for rising above work and anxiety :
above self and our own needs and aims :
for the study of Thy Holy Word and the
lives of Thy Saints :
for the worship of our Father in Heaven :
for the examination of our hearts and lives :
for preparation for Eternity, and Thy judgment.

6. O God, who art never weary in Thy loving kindness to us,
> we mourn that we grow weary of Thy day and Thy service:
>> say when will it be done that we may buy and sell:
>> men make it a day of sloth, or work, or amusement.
>> we have in thoughtlessness sacrificed the rest of others:
>> have forgotten the needs of our servants,
>>> Thy claim on their worship.

7. O our Lord and Saviour, who alone art the Bread of Life,
> how little do we feed on Thee:
>> we come to Thy table with weak faith and doubting hearts:
>> prepare ourselves so slightly for it:
>> although Thou dost so lovingly invite us, we neglect it, absent ourselves without reason:
>> we sometimes partake carelessly, irreverently:
>> we make resolutions and straightway forget them:
>> we come without expecting new grace of Thee:
>> we depart without regret that we have missed it.

APPENDIX.

I.

THE REFORMATION CONFESSION OF SINS, 1525.

Heavenly Father, merciful and everlasting God, we acknowledge and confess before Thy Divine Majesty that we are poor miserable sinners, conceived and brought forth in sin and corruption. We are prone to all evil. We cannot, without Thee, do anything that is good. And we daily, and in many ways, transgress Thy holy commandments. Thereby we provoke Thine anger against us, and draw down upon ourselves, by Thy just judgment, death and destruction.

But, O Lord, we repent and are sorry from our hearts that we have so displeased Thee. We condemn ourselves and our misdoings, and pray that Thy grace may bring help to our distress and misery.

Be pleased, therefore, to have mercy upon us, O most gracious God and Father. Forgive us all our sins, through the holy sufferings of Thy dear Son, our Lord Jesus Christ. Forgive us our sins; and grant us now the gifts of Thy Holy Spirit. Increase these in us from day to day; so that we, acknowledging with our whole hearts our own unrighteousness, may truly repent us of the same; that sin may be destroyed in us; and that we may bring forth the fruits of righteousness and a pure life which are well pleasing unto Thee, through Jesus Christ. Amen.

HISTORICAL NOTE.

This Confession of Sins—"die offne Schuld," as it is called in German-speaking Reformed Churches—is ascribed to Œcolampadius, the friend of Zwingli, and the Reformer of Basel. It appears in the liturgy of the Protestant Church of Zürich, in 1525. It occurs in the French liturgy which was published by Calvin at Geneva, in 1541, but which had been drawn up by him previously, and had been used by Protestant pastors of Geneva for several years before it was printed. It is the second "Confession of Sins" in the "Book of Geneva," used in that city in the English Congregation of which John Knox was minister. It is first in the Scottish Book of Common Order. Calvin's Service-book, republished in Latin in 1545, was the chief source from which this Confession passed rapidly into use in the Reformed Church catholic, and even in several of the Lutheran Churches. It stands, for example, in the present Liturgy of the National Church of Würtemberg as the first Confession of Sins for Days of Fasting, being taken from the Service-book of the Church of the Palatinate. It appears in English, among other prayers, at the end of an edition of Sternhold and Hopkins' Psalms, in 1566, under the title of "A Confession for all Estates and Times." Some writers have erroneously ascribed it to Beza, who used it in a striking scene at the Colloquy of Poissy, in 1561.

This ancient Confession of Sins is used in the Waldensian Church, both in the Valleys and in Italy. It is repeated in all the various branches of the Church of Holland and of the Church of the Huguenots, both in the Old World and in the New. It stands in all the Swiss, all the French, all the Rhineland Liturgies to this day. For wellnigh four hundred years this Confession has been on the lips and in the heart of the Reformed Church all over the world.

The "General Confession" in the Anglican Communion Service, which appears in the first Prayer-book of Edward VI. (1549), is closely akin to the Reformation Confession of Sins, especially in the form given below, in which it appears in the document known as "Hermann's Consultation." The "General Confession" in the Morning and Evening Services of the Church of England is drawn, like much else in the Prayer-book, from Presbyterian sources. It comes from Calvin's Service-book of 1545 through the liturgies of Pollanus and Alasco. Comp. Bannerman, *Worship of the Presbyterian Church*, pp. 79, 80, and 113-119, with the references there given.

II.

THE CONFESSION OF SINS IN "HERMANN'S CONSULTATION," ed. 1545.[1]

"*How the Lord's Supper is to be celebrated.*"

"When the people are gathered together for this action (ad hanc actionem[2]), as it is in accordance with true piety, that, as often as we appear before God in His Church, we should before all things acknowledge and confess our sins, and pray for forgiveness; let the minister who is to dispense the Lord's Supper, when he comes to the altar, make confession in the name of the whole Church, and that in the German tongue, so that all may understand, after this manner:

[1] See statement at end of Preface regarding this interesting Reformation Service-book. The confession begins: "Omnipotens æterne Deus, Pater Domini nostri Jesu Christi, Creator rerum omnium, Judex cunctorum hominum, agnoscimus et deploramus nos in peccatis conceptos et natos."

[2] Comp. our old Scottish phrase, the Action Sermon.

"Almighty, Everlasting God, the Father of our Lord Jesus Christ, Maker of all things, Judge of all men, we acknowledge and lament that we were conceived and born in sins, and so are prone to all evil and averse to all that is truly good. We have transgressed Thy holy commandments without measure and without end, through contempt of Thee and of Thy Word, through distrust of Thy help and trust in ourselves and in worldly things, through evil impulses and actions, whereby we have most grievously offended against Thy Divine Majesty and against our fellows. We have thus more and more buried ourselves and lost ourselves even unto death eternal. This grieveth us to the very heart; and we pray Thee to forgive us for all the things wherein we have sinned against Thee. We beseech Thy help against the sin that dwelleth in us, and against Satan who ever stirreth it up. Save us from sinning further against Thee. Cover all our iniquities with the righteousness of Thy Son. Subdue them in us by Thy Spirit, and cleanse us throughly from them in the end.

"Have mercy upon us, O most good and merciful Father, for Thy Son our Lord Jesus Christ's sake. Grant unto us, and increase in us, Thy Holy Spirit, that He may teach us inwardly and truly to acknowledge our sins, to mourn over them with lively repentance, and to receive and hold fast, with a true faith, the forgiveness of them in Christ our Lord, so that, dying daily more and more unto sin, we may serve and please Thee in newness of life, to the glory of Thy name, and the profit of Thy Church.

"These things we acknowledge that Thou justly requirest of us, wherefore we desire to do them. Be pleased, O Thou our Heavenly Father, who hast given us this desire, to grant also that we be diligent to do with our whole heart those things which pertain to our salvation, through Jesus Christ our Lord. Amen."

(Comfortable Words.)

Hear the Gospel from John iii. 16.

God so loved the world that He gave His only begotten Son, that whosoever believeth in Him should not perish, but have everlasting life.

Or from 1 Tim. i. 15.

This is a faithful saying, and worthy of all acceptation, that Christ Jesus came into the world to save sinners.

Or from John iii. 35 and 36.

The Father loveth the Son, and hath given all things into His hand. He that believeth on the Son hath everlasting life.

Or from Acts x. 43.

Unto Christ give all the prophets witness, that through His name whosoever believeth in Him shall receive remission of sins.

Or from 1 John ii. 1 and 2.

My little children, if any man sin we have an Advocate with the Father, Jesus Christ the righteous; and He is the propitiation for our sins.

(Absolution.)

When the pastor shall have proclaimed one of these Gospel words to the people, he shall add:

38 *ORDINARY SERVICE OF LORD'S DAY.* [PT. I.

Seeing that our blessed Lord hath left this power unto His Church that she should absolve from their sins, and restore to the grace of our heavenly Father, all those who repent of their sins, and truly believe in Christ our Lord; I, as a minister of Christ and of His Church, do now declare unto all here present whose sins are grievous unto them, and who truly believe in Christ our Lord, and desire to follow Him as His disciples, the forgiveness of all their sins, the grace of God, and life everlasting, through our Lord Jesus Christ. Amen.

Section III.

PETITION.

The order of the Petitions in the Lord's Prayer has been followed in the arrangement of the following materials and suggestions for Petition.

The subdivisions are mainly those of the Larger Catechism. Different sources have been used, especially the Book of Psalms, the devotional writings of Augustine, and those of Jeremy Taylor. The collection here presented is but the gleanings of a field which is practically as wide as human life itself.

Two short Litanies have been added, one of prayer to Christ, and one to the Holy Spirit.[1] Reference may also be made to the first part of Bucer's Litany, given below in Appendix to "Intercession."

---

[1] These are taken, with one or two slight verbal changes, from Fosbery's "Voices of Comfort," 3rd ed. pp. 56, 248.

I.—Our Father.

1. Give us Trust and Assurance.

Almighty God, our heavenly Father,

Grant that we may leave all things in Thy care, commit our way and our happiness to Thy keeping, and be content to fill a little space for Thy glory.

Grant that, knowing our ignorance and weakness, we may rely on Thy wisdom and strength.

The Lord is my rock, and my fortress, and my deliverer: my God, my strength, in whom I will trust.

O Thou who art the confidence of all the ends of the earth, be Thou our hope now and evermore, and our portion in the land of the living.

I will say of the Lord, He is my refuge and my fortress, my God, in Him will I trust.

How excellent is Thy loving-kindness, O Lord, therefore the children of men put their trust under the shadow of Thy wings.

2. Inspire us.

Most gracious Father,

Unto Thee do we lift up our souls.

O God, light of the hearts that see Thee, life of the souls that love Thee, strength of the thoughts that seek Thee, grant that with a holy love we may cleave to Thee.

As the hart panteth after the water-brooks, so panteth my soul after Thee, O God. My soul thirsteth for God, for the living God.

When the shadows lengthen upon our path, and sorrow rests upon our heart, O reveal Thyself in mercy.

Why art thou cast down, O my soul? and why art

thou disquieted within me? Hope in God, for I shall yet praise Him Who is the health of my countenance and my God.

3. **Grant us joy in God.**

Let all those that put their trust in Thee, rejoice; let them also that love Thy name, be joyful in Thee.
O satisfy us early with Thy mercy that we may rejoice and be glad all our days.
Grant that we may have the joy of those who are redeemed,
> that our days may be bright with gladness, because of Thy love,

Fill us with joy even when we fall into trial, because Thy strength is made perfect in our weakness.

II.—Hallowed be Thy Name.

1. **We beseech Thee, shew us Thy glory.**

Who shall not fear Thee, O Lord, and glorify Thy name.
Bless the Lord, O my soul, and all that is within me, bless His holy name.
O Lord our God, how excellent is Thy name in all the earth.
O God, who art the Giver of all good, grant that we may praise Thee, with penitence, purity, and gladness of heart.
Give us great and solemn apprehensions of Thy glory and power, of Thy majesty and mercy that we may adore Thee as our Creator and love thee as our Redeemer.
O Thou who art the Author and Fountain of all perfection, teach us to praise Thee.
Give us hearts bold, constant and valiant to confess Thee before the world, that we may choose rather

to suffer shame and loss than stain our conscience or renounce Thee.

Grant that the name of our Lord Jesus Christ may be glorified in us and we in Him.

Blessing and honour and glory and power be unto Him that sitteth upon the throne and unto the Lamb for ever and ever.

2. May we glorify Thee in our daily life.

Grant that all we do, say, or think may be to Thy glory,
> that men seeing our deeds may glorify Thee,
>> that by our life, men may grow stronger in faith, purer in thought, nobler in action,
>> that we may glorify God in our body and in our spirit which are thine,
>> that we may bring honour to Thy name by walking in the footsteps of Christ in all lowliness and meekness.

Let not our outward mercies make us careless of Thy service and honour.

III.—Thy Kingdom Come.

1. Overthrow the Kingdom of Sin.

O Lord God, who reignest a great King in all the earth, let Thy grace break down all the strongholds of sin and Satan.

O let the wickedness of the wicked come to an end, but establish the just.

Have respect unto the covenant, for the dark places of the earth are full of the habitations of cruelty.

Subdue in us every evil desire and inordinate affection, deliver us from pride and from all inward rebellion and repining of heart.

2. Spread the Knowledge of the Gospel.

God, be merciful unto us, and bless us, and cause Thy face to shine upon us, that Thy way may be known upon earth, &c.

Ask of Me and I shall give Thee the heathen for Thine inheritance, and the uttermost parts of the earth for Thy possession.

He shall come down like rain upon the mown grass, as showers that water the earth. He shall have dominion also from sea to sea; all nations shall call Him blessed.

Let all nations come and worship Thee, laying their proud wills at Thy feet, submitting themselves to the obedience of Christ, and conforming their affections to Thy holy laws.

Let the sound of the Gospel go into all the earth, may Thy people everywhere be ministers of Thy Kingdom, advancing Thy honour and furthering the salvation of all men.

Grant that all nations may fear Thee and give Thee praise, so that when Thou shalt come to judge the world they may receive Thy everlasting mercies.

Extend Thy blessings and Thy dominion from sea to sea, even unto the world's end, that all kings of the earth may fall down before Thee, and all nations do Thee service.

3. Edify and Equip Thy Church.

O blessed Lord, the rock upon whom Thy Church is built, be unto us a fountain of comfort when our hearts are in heaviness.

Thou shalt arise and have mercy on Zion ; for the time to favour her is come.

Pray for the peace of Jerusalem : they shall prosper that love thee. Peace be within thy walls, and prosperity within Thy palaces.

Be pleased, according to Thy gracious promise, to uphold Thy Church for ever ; let not the gates of hell prevail against her.

O God, Whose mercy reacheth unto the heavens, in mercy teach us to abhor everything that is evil, and to set ourselves in every good way.

Send a gracious rain, even the dew of Thy divine favour, upon Thine inheritance to refresh us in our weariness.

4. May Thy Saints be Confirmed, Comforted, Encouraged.

O Lord, Who art the health of our countenance and our God, when our hearts are cast down and disquieted within us, pity and comfort us.

Comfort and encourage us by the expectation of those glories which Thou hast laid up for them that love the appearing of our Lord.

Bring us at last to Thine eternal Kingdom, where no enemies shall assault or disturb our peace.

Grant that we may dwell with Thee for ever, and rejoice in the blessings of Thy Kingdom, who livest and reignest for ever one God, world without end.

Grant that we may all live before Thee in righteousness, waiting for the great day of Christ's appearance, and that we may not be ashamed before Him at His coming.

O Lord God, who dwellest in Zion, and delightest to have Thy habitation in the hearts of men, make us fit for Thy abiding.

IV.—Thy Will be Done.

1. That we may know Thy Will.

Open Thou mine eyes that I may behold wondrous things out of Thy law.

Cause me to hear Thy loving-kindness in the morning, for in Thee do I trust; cause me to know the way wherein I should walk, for I lift my soul unto Thee.

May my whole spirit, my whole heart, my whole life live to Thee Who art my life.

What thou hatest in me put far from me, and implant within me a spirit of purity and self-restraint, that nothing I desire may offend Thee.

May no selfish passion hinder us from knowing Thy will, and no weakness from doing it.

May we love to sit at Thy feet, and hearken to Thy holy words.

Open every window of our souls, that we may be full of light, and see the excellency of the love of Christ, and the merits of His sacrifice.

2. That we may do it.

O eternal God, Who hast made all things for man and man for Thy glory, sanctify our body and soul, our thoughts and intentions, our words and actions, that all we think, or speak, or do may be to the glory of Thy name.

O that my ways were directed to keep Thy statutes;

with my whole heart have I sought Thee; O let me not wander from Thy commandments.

Teach me to do Thy will, for Thou art my God.

Teach me, O Lord, the way of Thy statutes, and I shall keep it to the end.

O eternal God, fountain of all truth and holiness, take from us all disobedience and perversity of spirit, all ambition, all private and base interests.

Remove from us all prejudice, and strengthen in us all true conviction, that we may resign ourselves to Thy persuasion.

Thy will is the measure of our holiness and peace; make it also the measure of our desires.

Grant that the Spirit of Grace may draw us to Him Who is meek and lowly, that we may take His yoke upon us and learn of Him.

O that in every passage of life we may reflect on Thy example and copy Thee.

Thou who workest in us, both to will and to do of Thy good pleasure, teach us to obey all Thy commandments.

Grant that we may imitate the holy example of our Lord Jesus Christ, and renounce our wills for Thine.

3. **That we may Submit to it.**

O Thou who didst bear the burden of the cross, be pleased to lighten our load by strengthening our spirit.

Thy ways are a great deep and not to be searched out. O teach us to submit to Thy will in all things.

Teach us to be content in all changes, to read our duty in Thy Providence, and in adversity to be steadfast, patient, hopeful.

Give us grace to say from the heart, "Thy will, not mine, be done."

Grant that the yoke of Christ may become easy to us, and His burden light.

5. That we may be humble.

O holy and most gracious Master, Who by Thy example and Thy precept didst command us to be meek and humble, be pleased to give us the grace as Thou hast given the commandment.

Give what Thou commandest, and command what Thou wilt.

Teach us to imitate the gracious condescension of Thy Son when He washed His disciples' feet.

When we are praised for doing our duty, grant that we may give the glory to Thee, and remember that Thou knowest our imperfections.

Save us from all proud thoughts and vain opinions of ourselves.

Keep us from boasting ourselves of what Thou hast freely bestowed.

May our glory be in the Cross of Christ and the lowly service of men, that so thinking little of ourselves we may be honoured by Thee.

6. **Faithfulness.** 8. **Sincerity.**
7. **Zeal.** 9. **Constancy.**

V.—GIVE US EACH DAY OUR DAILY BREAD.

1. That we may wait on God's Providence.

O Thou upon whom the eyes of all do wait, give unto us our meat in due season. Open Thou Thine hand and satisfy the desire of every living thing.

O God, the giver of every good and every perfect gift, keep us from all distrust of Thy providence, and all doubtings of Thy kindness and care.

O God, Who art the portion of our inheritance, preserve and maintain all those good things which Thou hast wrought in us and for us.

O merciful Father, Who hast the keys of life and death, dispose of us as Thou pleasest and give us grace to trust Thee always.

2. That we may enjoy God's goodness.

O God, the hope of all the ends of the earth, make the earth plenteous and bless the increase of it; crown the year with Thy goodness.

Let Thy loving-kindness and mercy follow us all our days that we may dwell in Thy house for ever.

O blessed Jesus, Thou great Shepherd and Bishop of our souls, feed us with the Word and Sacraments, and refresh us with the comforts of Thy Holy Spirit.

Grant that we being refreshed with the multitude of Thy blessings may praise Thee, and at last be satisfied with the pleasures of Thy house where Thou livest and reignest one God world without end.

3. That we may trust in God's care.

O Thou Who hast clothed the flowers with glory greater than Solomon's, and feedest the birds of the air, teach us that we are more precious in Thy sight than they, and that Thou wilt care for us with a Father's care.

Give us grace to think little of earthly things and to put our trust in Thee.

Teach us to lay up our treasure in heaven by charity and actions of piety: unmoved by the terrors of the world: unaltered by its allurements and seduction: not ambitious of its honours or wealth.

Grant that we may not place our joys and hopes upon the good things of this life which perish and cannot satisfy, but in the eternal fountain of all true felicities.

O God, from whom all grace and safety and glory do proceed, hear our prayers whenever we call upon Thee in our trouble, for our trust is in Thee alone.

4. That we be Contented.

O Lord our God, let no riches make us ever forget ourselves and no poverty ever make us forget Thee.

Let us never envy any man's goods, nor deserve to be despised ourselves.

Give us neither poverty nor riches, feed us with food convenient for us.

Teach us to think lightly of the world, to labour for the true riches, and to be content with what Thou providest.

Grant that we may never envy the prosperity of anyone, but rejoice to honour him whom Thou honourest, and to love him whom Thou lovest.

Let it not be ill with us when it is well with others; but grant that we may promote their good and give Thee thanks for it.

Let the employment of our day leave no sorrow, nor the remembrance of it an evil conscience at night.

5. That we may have the Spirit of Christ.

Conform our mind and will to Thy holy precepts, that we may imitate Thy Son in all things:

His devotion in prayer, His obedience to Thee,
His zeal tempered with meekness,
His patience heightened with charity.
That we may ever grow in grace till we come to the measure of the fulness of the stature in Christ.

VI.—Forgive us our Debts.

1. **Acquit us.**

Have patience with us, O Lord, yet as we have not wherewith to pay, forgive us the whole debt, we beseech Thee.

By the riches of Thy grace, by the exceeding abundance of Thy mercy, by the great love wherewith Thou hast loved us, be merciful to us sinners—to us of all sinners the greatest, the most wretched.

Lord, remit the guilt, heal the wound, blot out the stains, deliver from the shame and from the tyranny of our sin.

Pardon all our sins, our foolish and rash words, the vanity and worldliness of our thoughts, our unjust and uncharitable actions, and whatsoever we have done against Thee this day.

Have mercy upon us, O Lord, according to Thy lovingkindness; according unto the multitude of Thy tender mercies, blot out our transgressions.

2. **Pardon our daily failings and keep us from sin.**

Most gracious God, if Thou permittest us at any time to fall, let us not sleep in sin, but recall us by conscience and the working of Thy Holy Spirit.

Uphold us, that we may not fall again into those great sins by which we have so offended against Thee.

Let our hearts be so cleansed and kept by Thy grace that we may never, by deliberation and purpose, or by levity and thoughtlessness, sin against Thee.

Let Thy Spirit keep us in all our ways from the occasions and opportunities of evil, from all the paths of shame, from a sinful life, and from despair in the hour of death.

Let us not continue our days in folly and vanity, lest our years be spent in trouble.

When, through infirmity, we fall, let Thy gentle correction call us home, that we may turn us early and seek after Thee Who art our God.

3. Give us peace, joy, assurance.

O Thou God of peace, grant that our peace may be in a good conscience, and our joy in Thee.

Grant that, since Thou alone art our treasure, our hearts may be fixed upon Thee by the bonds of love and obedience.

Restore unto us the joy of Thy salvation, and uphold us in a free spirit.

Build our faith upon Thy promises in Jesus Christ, and our hopes upon Thy goodness and mercy.

Lead us from grace to grace, from imperfection to strength, and from effort to glory.

Give us the assistance of Thy grace, that we may always walk before Thee without offence, fearing even the approach of sin.

4. Give us grace to forgive others.

O God, Who delightest in mercy, give us merciful hearts,
    that we may forgive even as we are forgiven:
        that we may suffer with suffering men;

that we may do all things, and bear all things, to deliver them from misery or sin.

O God, who didst love us while we were enemies, teach us to love those that hate us,
> do good to those that wrong us, and offer all kindness, tenderness, and relief to our enemies.

Enable us to take Thy mercy for the pattern and measure of our forbearance.

Give us a readiness to bear each other's burdens, a spirit of meekness and modesty, trembling at our own infirmities, fearful in our brother's dangers and joyful in his success.

Give us a great love, that we may truly forgive all that trouble or injure us.

Give us a meek and gentle spirit, that we may be easy to be entreated to mercy and forgiveness.

VII.—LEAD US NOT INTO TEMPTATION.

1. **Subdue the world, the flesh, and the devil.**

From sin and shame, from the malice and fraud of the devil, from the falseness and greed of men, from all Thy wrath, and from all our impurities, good Lord, deliver us. From the lust of the flesh, the lust of the eye, and the pride of life; from earthly mindedness and frivolity, from all indolence in holy things, from all unbelief and hardness of heart, &c. &c., good Lord, deliver us.

Make haste and help us, O God, against all these that seek after our souls to destroy them.

To this day and all days, vouchsafe, O Lord, a perfect, holy, peaceful, sinless course.

Thou Who upholdest the falling and liftest the fallen, let us not harden our hearts in provocation, or temptation, or in any deceitfulness of sin.
Deliver us from the recollection of evil things.

2. Strengthen us in temptation.

Be not far from us, when trouble is near, and there is none to help; O, our Strength, haste Thee to help us.
Hold up our goings in Thy paths, that our footsteps slip not.
Thou art our hiding-place; Thou shalt preserve us from trouble; Thou shalt compass us about with songs of deliverance.
Suffer us not to be tempted above that we are able.
O God, the Giver of all grace and the Author of all spiritual strength, strengthen us so with Thy grace that we may fight a good fight and conquer, and be crowned with a crown of righteousness.
When Thou shalt try us and suffer us to be tempted, be on our side, that we may fight valiantly, endure patiently, and persevere unto the end.
Leave us not, neither forsake us, when we are assaulted by enemies without and temptations within.

3. Perfect us through temptation.

Grant, O most merciful Father, that even our temptations may tend to make us perfect and entire.
O gracious Saviour, do Thou plead for us when we are tempted, that our faith fail not, but rather be strengthened.
Grant that the trying of our faith may be found unto

praise and glory and honour at the revelation of Jesus Christ.

May the memory of the temptation, and the sufferings of our Lord and Saviour, teach us to rejoice in ours.

O God, Who art faithful, and Who wilt with the temptation make a way of escape, grant that we may be able not only to endure, but to reach a higher grace.

4. **Make us watchful against temptation.**

Teach us to give most earnest heed lest we drift away from Thee.

Set Thou a watch before our mouth, that we sin not with our lips.

Teach us to watch over all our ways, that we may never be surprised by sudden temptation.

Give us a wise and watchful spirit, that we may omit no opportunity of serving Thee.

Give us watchfulness over our words, that we speak no guile, and over our actions that we eschew all evil.

5. **May Christ reign in our hearts.**

Grant that our affections be guided by the mind of Christ, our understandings enlightened by His word, our wills persuaded and strengthened by His Spirit, and that in our lives we may be made perfect as He is.

Be pleased to enter into our souls with triumph, trampling down all Thine enemies.

Give us grace to entertain Thee with joy and adoration.

Take captive our thoughts and desires and imaginations.

Bind us with bands of love, so that our union with Thee may break the bands of sin.

Give us grace to look for Thy coming in humility and love.

When Thy Kingdom is established within us, grant that Thy Kingdom of Glory may come speedily.

VIII.—Deliver us from Evil.

1. Overrule the ills of life for our good.

O merciful Jesus, Who for our sakes didst suffer Thyself to be betrayed, tormented, spit upon, crucified, and to die that Thou mightest purchase redemption for us, deliver our souls from evil.

Let those victories which Thou hast obtained over Satan, and hell, and the grave, bring us peace and righteousness, and victory over our enemies, and a crown of glory in the heavens.

Thou shalt compass us about with songs of deliverance.

O Lord, command Thy loving-kindness in the day-time, and in the night let Thy song be with us, and our prayer unto the God of our life.

Let strength be made perfect in weakness.

Let nothing separate us from Thy love, which is in Jesus Christ our Lord.

2. Give courage amid the ills of life.

God is our refuge and strength, a very present help in trouble.

From the end of the earth will we cry unto Thee when our heart is overwhelmed. Lead us to the rock that is higher than we.

O Lord, Who art a merciful High Priest and art touched with a feeling of our infirmities, let Thy mercy support us and Thy Spirit guide us.

In the midst of darkness, make us strong in the Lord, in hope of pardon, in expectation of glory and in the sense of Thy mercies.

Assure us that Thou wilt hide us under the shadow of Thy wings, and hold up our goings in Thy paths that our footsteps slip not.

3. Give victory in trial, suffering, sorrow.

In the midst of our afflictions, teach us to remember Thine, O our Master, that we may bear them patiently and gain Thy victory over all.

By Thine agony and bloody sweat: by Thy cross and passion, good Lord, deliver us.

When Thou Who art the Head wast crowned with thorns, shall we Thy unworthy members live at ease? Shall we complain of our hardships when Thou hadst not where to lay Thy head?

Try us as gold is tried: and as a refiner do Thou purify us.

Let neither hope nor fear, tribulation nor anguish, pleasure nor sorrow separate us from Thy love.

We wear the badge of a crucified Saviour, grant that we shrink not back at every cross we meet.

Let no sickness or cross, no employment or weariness make us angry or ungentle, discontented or unthankful.

Grant that when Thou hast tried us as silver is tried, we may come forth pure and fit for Thy holy service.

Let Thy merciful hand lead us through the fire of our affliction that we may not be consumed.

IX.—Thine is the Kingdom and the Power and the Glory for ever.

O Lord God our strength, Whose mercies are infinite, Whose majesty is glorious, Whose goodness is above all that is good on earth, enlarge our hearts with joy and rejoicing in Thy glories.

Grant that we, looking for Thee in holiness of living, longing and thirsting after Thee with fervent desires, may for ever behold Thy power and glory, and our life and hearts praise Thee to all eternity.

Grant that we may tell of Thy greatness and declare Thy salvation from day to day.

Grant that when Thou comest with righteousness to judge the earth and all people with Thy truth, we may rejoice in Thee everlastingly.

O Great God, King of Heaven and Earth, Thou that sittest between the cherubim, give unto us an adoration of the sanctity and perfections of Thy name, which is great and wonderful and holy.

Let a sense of Thy dread majesty check every irreverent thought in us, and teach us to make our approach unto Thee in humility and fear.

APPENDIX.

I.

Litany, chiefly to Christ.

O God, the Father of Heaven: O God, the Son, Redeemer of the world; O God, the Holy Ghost, the Comforter; O holy, blessed, and glorious Trinity:

Have mercy upon us.

O Lord Jesus Christ, who for us didst endure a life of suffering upon earth:
Give us grace to take up our cross and follow Thee.

O Lord Jesus Christ, who was lifted up from the earth that Thou mightest draw all men unto Thee:
Draw us also unto Thyself.

By Thy fasting and temptation, Thy homeless wanderings, Thy lonely watchings on the mountains; by the weariness and painfulness of Thy ministry among men:
Good Lord, deliver us.

By Thine unknown sorrows and sufferings; by Thine agony and bloody sweat; by Thy cross and passion; by the power of Thy blood shed for sinners:
Good Lord, deliver us.

We sinners do beseech Thee to hear us, that we, being dead unto sin, may live unto righteousness:
We beseech Thee to hear us, good Lord.

That we may be ready to endure hardness as good soldiers of Jesus Christ:
We beseech Thee to hear us, good Lord.

That we may use this world, as not abusing it:
We beseech Thee to hear us, good Lord.

That our hearts may be wholly Thine in prosperity as in adversity:
We beseech Thee to hear us, good Lord.

Our Father which art in heaven, Hallowed be Thy name. . . .

II.

Litany to the Holy Spirit.

O God, the Holy Ghost, proceeding from the Father and the Son:
Have mercy upon us.

O Holy Spirit, Comforter of the weary and the sad:
Comfort us, we beseech Thee, in all our tribulations.

O Holy Spirit, Illuminator of Thy people:
Give us light, we beseech Thee, in the darkness of this world.

O Holy Spirit, Sanctifier of Thine elect:
Keep us, we beseech Thee, from all sin.

O Holy Spirit, Advocate with the Father:
Intercede for us, we beseech Thee, according to the will of God.

O Holy Spirit of Love:
Teach us, we beseech Thee, more and more of the love of Christ.

O Holy Spirit of Truth:
Lead us, we beseech Thee, into all truth, and bring always to our remembrance the words of Jesus.

O Holy Spirit of Counsel:
Guide us, we beseech Thee, through the trials and perplexities of life.

O blessed Spirit, who art the Lord and the Giver of Life, dwell with us and in us, according to our Saviour's own promise. Without Thee we are as orphans in this world; leave us not comfortless, we beseech Thee. We are poor and needy; we know not what we should pray for as we ought; pray Thou for us, we beseech Thee, according to the will of God. Help our infirmities—Purify our hearts—Breathe into our souls ever more the breath of Thy Divine life; that our whole body and soul and spirit may be made and kept blameless, unto the coming of our Lord Jesus Christ. We ask all for His sake. AMEN.

Section IV.

THANKSGIVING.

THERE must be many in every congregation who come to church in a spirit that can hardly be called devotional; and perhaps the least common mood even for a devotional spirit is that of thanksgiving. We are all more or less conscious of our sins and of our wants; but it is with an effort that we recall our mercies. One of the difficulties, therefore, of public prayer must be to evoke gratitude in the heart of the worshipper. Again, we cannot well do it by general expressions of thanks. A prayer of general thanksgiving, however fine and impressive it may be to a spiritual mind, often seems to minds not spiritual only exaggerated and unreal. Its power is due to its touching chords that are sensitive and quick to respond, to its awakening memories that have been often renewed and are never far to seek. In order to do a like service to the less devout, we must mention and dwell upon the special mercies of God, we must touch those points of their life where they cannot but acknowledge the hand of a loving Father. As we all learn to know the sinfulness of our hearts only through individual acts of sin, so we learn to be thankful through perceiving the specific acts of God's goodness in our daily lives. By specifying them in prayer, then, we awaken memories in hearts dull and slow, and by means of that lift them to gratitude and the ascription of all praise to the Giver of all good.

The combining of the general and the special thanksgiving will take very different forms with different men; but because we tend to neglect the details of mercy, so necessary for the devotion of the ordinary Christian, or to a monotonous repetition of the more striking among them, greater space has been given to the "Enumeration of Mercies," than to general expressions of thanks. They are but specimens of the rich materials that lie ready to our hands.

The sections have been taken from many sources —Bishop Andrews, Jeremy Taylor, Dr Hunter, &c., and have been modified quite freely to suit our purpose.

I.—Forms.

For . . . . . . { We praise Thee, O God.
                    We thank and praise Thee.
For all Thy . . . We praise Thy holy name.

Blessed art Thou who . . .

Glory be to Thee who . . .

Blessed be Thy holy name for . . .

Thou art worthy to receive praise, for . . .

Accept our thanks for all Thy . . .

II.—General Thanksgiving.

It is a good thing to give thanks unto the Lord, and to sing praises unto Thy name, O most high: to show forth Thy loving-kindness in the morning and Thy faithfulness every night.

We will extol Thee, our God, O King, and praise Thy name for ever and ever. Every day will we bless Thee, and we will praise Thy name for ever and ever.

Great is the Lord and greatly to be praised, and His greatness is unsearchable. One generation shall praise Thy works to another, and shall declare Thy mighty acts.

We will speak of the glorious honour of Thy majesty and of Thy wondrous works. Men shall speak of the might of Thy terrible acts: and we will declare Thy greatness.

O Lord, Thou art good to all: and Thy tender mercies are over all Thy works.

All Thy works shall praise Thee, O Lord, and Thy saints shall bless Thee.

The eyes of all wait upon Thee, and Thou givest them their meat in due season. Thou openest Thine hand and satisfiest the desire of every living thing.

While we live we will praise Thee, O Lord: we will sing praises unto Thee, our God, while we have any being.

&c., &c.

III.—Enumeration of Mercies.

1. For our birth and being:
    born in a land where Thy name is feared:
    where we are free to read Thy holy word:
    where we can worship and serve Thee in peace:
    in homes where prayer was daily offered to Thee:
    where we were sheltered from temptation:
    where we were trained to reverence and love Thee.

2. That Thou madest us but a little lower than the angels:
    able to understand something of Thy way:
    able to love Thee, obey Thee, help Thee:
    that Thou hast blest us with a knowledge of Thyself:
    given us Reason that we may think Thy thoughts, follow Thy wondrous working:
    hearts that are pained by wrong, and made glad by kindness:
    wills that can be conformed to Thine:
    souls that are made strong by service, and changed into the likeness of Christ by faith and love,

3. For our Education:
    by men who loved righteousness, truth, honour:
    who taught us to scorn idleness, deceit, cruelty, vice:
    who taught us to seek Thee and Thy help:
    to trust Thy mercy and Thy care.

> to live not for ourselves but for Christ and our fellow-men:
> to rejoice in the glory and the beauty of Thy works:
> to find pleasure in what is lovely and true and good in books, art, noble activities of men.

4. For Thy Preservation of us:
   in times of danger when our companions fell:
   when no eye was watching over us but Thine:
   when as children Thou didst take us into Thine arms, put Thy hands upon us and bless us:
   when the pestilence walked in darkness:
   covered with Thy feathers:
   led us beside still waters.

5. For our Friends:
   who strengthened our hands when we were weak:
   > pointed us to higher duties and nobler lives:
   > encouraged us when faint-hearted:
   > quickened our hearts, purified our minds:
   > rebuked our vanity, our uncharitable judgments:
   > taught us to scorn baseness and to fear sin.

6. For our daily work:
   that has taught us perseverance:
   > helped us to forget ourselves:
   > taught us to seek higher ends than self:

>> healed our wounds and soothed our sorrows:
>> made us helpers of Almighty God.

7. For the world:
    its unending beauty:
    for the glories of the day and of the night:
    >> summer and winter, seed-time and harvest:
    for Thy works so unsearchable:
    >> Thy glory in the heavens, earth, and sea.

8. For the gift of Thy Son:
    Thine eternal purpose of grace:
    the great love wherewith Thou hast loved us:
    Christ's lowly birth in a manger:
    His patient toil as a working man:
    His obedience that has taught us how to obey:
    His loving service of the humblest and the worst:
    His temptation, giving us courage to draw near, and hope to struggle on:
    His weariness, teaching us patience:
    His sufferings, that give us victory over ours:
    that when reviled, He reviled not again:
    >> when mocked, He was silent:
    >> when hated, He loved the more:
    >> when condemned, He endured:
    >> when crucified, He blessed and prayed for enemies.

    for all the good deeds He did, loving words He spoke, which now give hope to the hopeless and life to the dead:
    for His prayers in behalf of friends and enemies:

THANKSGIVING.   [SEC. IV.] 65

    His example in days of quietness and of disaster :
    His gentleness to the base and the rude :
    His agony in Gethsemane :
    His sufferings on Calvary that have saved the world :
    His resurrection, giving us a living hope.

9. For Thy Holy Spirit :
    all His guidance of Thy people in the past—of us to-day :
    His taking the things of Christ and shewing them to us :
    every holy thought that comes to our mind :
    every aspiration after a worthier life :
    every struggle against self and sin :
    every endeavour to attain the likeness of Christ :
    our times of deep repentance :
        hours of communion :
        moments of silent prayer :
        visions of a life spent for God and man :
        resolutions and vows to follow Christ.

10. For opportunity of Christian work :
    our desires to do something for Christ :
        to be fellow-workers with Thee for men :
    our power to speak Thy truth :
        tell the wonders of Thy grace :
        labour and suffer for Christ :
    every opportunity of manifesting Thy grace in our hearts :
    every gift dedicated to Thy service :

every word spoken gently to the tried and tempted :
spoken bravely against iniquity :
every cup of cold water given in Christ's name.

11. For the discipline of life:
trials that have trained us to patience :
temptations that have taught us to trust only in Thy strength :
troubles that lift us nearer to Thee :
wrongs, insults, slights, that we have been able to bear patiently in the Spirit of Christ :
burdens that have forced us to turn to Thee for help :
enmity of men that has brought us to Thee in prayer :
sorrows that have lifted our treasure to Heaven and set our affection on things above :
sacred ties that bind us to the world unseen :
faith that walks without fear through the valley of the shadow of death :
that sees beyond the darkness to the light eternal :
that can rest quietly in Thy arms even though the earth be shaking.

12. For Thy calling of us
out of sin—from the power of Satan unto God :
into the fellowship of Thy Son Jesus Christ, our Lord :
calling not the wise and mighty and noble only,

but the poor and contrite and broken-hearted:
convincing us of the sinfulness of sin:
of the misery of a life spent apart from Thee:
for the prize of Thy high calling:
calling us to the very perfection of our Father:
calling us into the peace of God:
into lowliness and meekness of Jesus:
to obtain the glory of our Lord.

13. For the lives of Thy saints:
every one whose faith was strong:
in whose heart was charity:
the patriarchs and their faith:
the prophets and their unquenchable hope:
the apostles and their unwearied labours:
the evangelists and their gospel of Thy Son:
the martyrs and their courage, endurance, blood
the confessors and their zeal.

every sinner whom Thou hast saved:
the publican who left all and followed Thee
the thief who on the cross prayed to Thee.

14. Blessed be Thy name, O holy Jesus, for
Thou wentest about doing good:
working miracles of mercy, healing the sick:
comforting the distressed, instructing the ignorant:
raising the dead, enlightening the blind:
reconciling sinners by the mightiness of Thy loving power.

15. Blessed be Thy name, O holy Jesus,
    content to be conspired against by Thine own people:
    to be sold for money by a disciple:
    to wash the feet of Him who was betraying Thee:
    to sit near Him and give Him bread and wine:
    to become a sacrifice for the sins of men—even for the sin of their betrayal and denial and forsaking Thee:
    for all our sins who have betrayed Thee, and denied Thee, and crucified Thee afresh:
    for sins we should be afraid to think of, but that their greatness reveals the greatness of Thy mercy.

16. Blessed be Thy holy name, O patient and loving Lord,
    who, when Thy disciple denied Thee, and forsook Thee, and forswore Thee, didst look upon him and by Thy gracious and chiding look didst call him to himself and Thee:
    who wert found without fault and yet sentenced to death:
    who, when malice roared about Thee like a stormy sea, wert calm and silent and forgiving.

17. Blessed be Thy name, O holy Jesus, and blessed be Thy patience and love
    by which Thou wert content that that face which angels with wonder do behold, should be spit upon by men:

content that Barabbas should be counted worthier and preferred to Thee:
that Thou shouldst be struck and mocked and scourged and crushed under the weight of Thy cross, and yet shouldst pity not Thyself, but the women weeping beside Thee.

18. Blessed be Thy name, O holy Jesus, and blessed be Thy holy sorrow which Thou sufferedst for us:
that Thou prayedst for Thy murderers:
that Thou wouldst not soothe Thy sufferings, but didst drink the cup Thy Father gave Thee to the dregs:

Lord what is man that Thou shouldst be thus mindful of him or the son of man that Thou shouldst thus visit him?

APPENDIX.

I.

Thou art worthy, O Lord, to receive glory and honour and power, for Thou hast created all things, and for Thy pleasure they are and were created. O Lord, open Thou our lips, and our mouth shall show forth Thy praise.

Our soul doth praise Thee, for the goodness Thou hast done to the whole race of men; for Thy mercies towards us, in soul and body and estate; for Thy gifts of grace, and nature, and fortune; for all benefits received; for all successes, now or heretofore; for any good thing done; for health, credit, competency, safety, gentle estate, quiet. Thou holdest our soul in life, and sufferest not our feet to slip. Thou hast rescued us from perils, sicknesses, poverty, bondage, public shame, evil chances. Thou hast kept us from perishing in our sins, patiently waited our conversion, left in us return into our heart, remembrance of our latter end, shame, horror, grief, for our past sins. Fuller and larger, larger and fuller, more and still more, O our Lord, Thou hast stored us with good hope of their remission, through repentance and its works.

Wherefore day by day, for these Thy benefits towards us which we remember; and for very many which we have let slip, from their number and from our forgetfulness: for those which we wished and knew, and asked, and those we asked not, knew not, wished not, we give thanks to Thee, we bless and praise Thee every day. Glory be to Thee, O Lord, glory to Thee for Thine incomprehensible goodness, and Thy pity towards sinful and unworthy men, and towards us, of all sinners far the most unworthy. For this, O Lord, and for the rest, glory be to Thee, and praise, and blessing, and thanksgiving.

ANDREWS (*condensed*).

II.

O most merciful and gracious God, Thou fountain of all mercy and blessing, Thou hast opened the hand of Thy mercy to fill us with blessings, and the sweet effects of Thy loving-kindness; Thou feedest us like a shepherd,

THANKSGIVING.

Thou governest us as a king, Thou bearest us in Thy arms like a nurse, Thou dost cover us under the shadow of Thy wings and shelter us; Thou wakest for us like a watchman, Thou providest for us like a husband, Thou lovest us as a friend, and thinkest on us perpetually, as a careful mother on her helpless child, and art exceedingly merciful to all that fear Thee. And now, O Lord, Thou hast added this great blessing of deliverance from . . .; it was Thy hand and the help of Thy mercy that relieved us; the waters of affliction had drowned us, and the stream had gone over our soul, if the Spirit of the Lord had not moved upon these waters. Unto Thee, O Lord, we ascribe the praise and honour of our redemption. We will be glad and rejoice in Thy mercy, for Thou hast considered our trouble and hast known our soul in adversity. As Thou hast spread Thy hand upon us for a covering, so also enlarge our heart with thankfulness, and fill our mouth with praises, that our duty and returns to Thee may be great as our needs of mercy are: and let Thy gracious favours and loving-kindness endure for ever and ever upon Thy servants; and grant that what Thou hast sown in mercy may spring up in duty: and let Thy grace so strengthen our purposes, that we may sin no more, lest Thy threatening return upon us in anger, and Thy anger break us into pieces: but let us walk in the light of Thy favour, and in the paths of Thy commandments; that we, living here to the glory of Thy name, may at last enter into the glory of our Lord, to spend a whole eternity in giving praise to Thy exalted and ever glorious name.

JEREMY TAYLOR.

III.

A General Thanksgiving.

Almighty God, Father of all mercies, we Thine unworthy servants do give Thee most humble and hearty thanks for all Thy goodness and loving-kindness to us and to all men. We bless Thee for our creation, preservation, and all the blessings of this life; but above all, for Thine inestimable love in the redemption of the world by our Lord Jesus Christ; for the means of grace and for the hope of glory. And, we beseech Thee, give us that due sense of all Thy mercies, that our hearts may be unfeignedly thankful; and that we shew forth Thy praise, not only with our lips, but in our lives, by giving up ourselves to Thy service, and by walking before Thee in holiness and righteousness all our days; through Jesus Christ our Lord, to whom with Thee and the Holy Ghost be all honour and glory, world without end. Amen.

Historical Note.

The author of this beautiful prayer of thanksgiving was Dr Edward Reynolds, a very eminent divine of the seventeenth century, "the pride and glory of the Presbyterian party in the city of London," as Wood calls him. He was a member of the Westminster Assembly of Divines, and took a prominent part in all its work, being noted for the great regularity of his attendance. He was a Member of the Committee on the Catechism, of which Herbert Palmer, then Master of Queen's College, Cambridge, was chairman. Dr Reynolds was often appointed to preach before the Long Parliament, and held various important positions under their authority. He was made Dean of Christ

Church, Oxford, and Vice-Chancellor of the University there. After the Restoration, he became Bishop of Norwich, and died in 1676.[1]

There is some resemblance between his "General Thanksgiving" and part of a Thanksgiving Prayer ascribed to Queen Elizabeth.

IV.

THANKSGIVING BEFORE THE COMMUNION:—"VERE DIGNUM ET JUSTUM EST, ÆQUUM ET SALUTARE."

(from Hermann's "Consultation," slightly shortened and adapted.)

It is very meet and right, just and wholesome that we should at all times and in all places give thanks unto Thee, Holy Father, Almighty, Everlasting God, through Jesus Christ our Lord. We bless Thee that through Him Thou didst make us at the first in Thine image; and that when we, falling away from Thee through sin, had become Thine enemies, and so subject unto death and eternal judgment, Thou of Thine infinite mercy and love, didst send Thy Son to be our Saviour from sin and death and all the power of the devil. We thank and praise Thee for His Cross and Passion, for the Holy Ghost whom Thou didst send to us from Him, and that Thou hast made us in Him to be sons and daughters of the Lord Almighty. Wherefore, with all Thy holy angels and dear children, we would evermore praise Thee, saying: Holy, holy, holy, Lord God of hosts; heaven and earth are full of Thy glory: glory be to Thee, O Lord Most High. Amen.

[1] See Reid, *Memoirs of the Westminster Assembly Divines*, II. 128-131. Neal, *Hist. of the Puritans*, II. 487, III. 204.

V.

THANKSGIVING FOR THE COMMUNION OF SAINTS.

(from liturgy of German Reformed Church of America.)

O God, the Father of our Lord Jesus Christ, of whom the whole family in heaven and earth is named, we rejoice before Thee in the blessed communion of all Thy Saints, wherein Thou givest us also to have part. We praise Thee for the holy fellowship of patriarchs and prophets, apostles and martyrs, and the whole company of the redeemed of all ages, who died in the Lord, and now live with Him for evermore. We give thanks unto Thee for all Thy grace and goodness to them and for Thy gifts bestowed upon them. Enable us to follow their faith, that we may enter at death into their joy, and abide with them in rest and peace, until both they and we shall reach our common consummation of redemption and bliss in the glorious resurrection of the last Day, through Jesus Christ our Lord. Amen.

SECTION V.

INTERCESSION.

No part of public prayer is generally listened to with such attention and joined in with such readiness as Intercession. Everyone can follow it; for everyone understands the references, and probably has a personal interest in them. No part stimulates Christian affection and brotherly love so much. It is here that the sympathies of a congregation can be widened and deepened, and the most difficult of Christian graces—to forgive an enemy, and to be merciful as our Father in heaven is merciful—can be learned.

The edifying power of Intercession is incalculable; and for this reason much space has been assigned to it here, and both range of topic and variety of expression have been sought for.

Definiteness and variety of request form part of the strength and attractiveness of that fine form of the litany which is familiar to most of us in the Anglican Book of Common Prayer. Its weakness lies in its length, in a certain amount of needless repetition at the beginning and end, and, as regards the Anglican Church and its offshoots in America and elsewhere, in its being used without adaptation to times and circumstances, and to the exclusion of free prayer. A good illustration of this last point was given by the late Bishop Phillips Brooks of Massachusetts, when pleading before a congress of his own church (the American Episcopal) in behalf of greater freedom in prayer. A large Episcopal Convention was in session, he said, when they learned that the great city of Chicago was on fire, and that thousands of people were houseless and exposed to extreme danger. With a natural and praiseworthy impulse, all agreed that it was right to join in prayer for their fellow-countrymen suffering under such a calamity. The business in hand was adjourned accordingly; when, behold, a fatal difficulty emerged. There was no form of prayer in the liturgy for such a case, and it was, of course, impossible to depart from it. The assembled bishops and clergy had to content themselves with going devoutly over the litany, "laying before God almost every woe but the woe of a burning city!" "Surely,"

Dr Brooks said, "bishops, clergy, and laity should have liberty to pour out their souls to God, wherever they be, for the very things they need, instead of compelling them to go in a roundabout way, praying for other things, and trusting Omniscience to give them the things which are in their hearts!"

An older and shorter form of the litany is given in the Appendix. It was prepared by Bucer for Hermann's "Consultation" in 1543.

I.—For all Men.

O God who art the Hope of all the ends of the Earth,
Remember the whole Creation for good.
Pity our race whose portion is sin, and misery, and shame, and death.
Fulfil Thy purpose of love toward mankind.
Save this world for whom Thou gavest Thine only begotten Son.
Thou hast promised thy Son the nations for an inheritance, and the uttermost parts of the earth for His possession,
bring them speedily into His kingdom.
Grant that the nations of the Earth may no longer use their strength to work desolation: that all men may acknowledge Thou art King, and honour and obey Thee, world without end.

II.—Our Native Land.

Almighty God, on Whom our fathers hoped, and Thou didst deliver them,

1. Grant that religion and virtue may be found in all our land :
that there may be peace and plenty within our coast.
In peace, so preserve us that we grow not corrupt :
in plenty, grant that we be not proud and forget Thee :
in want, teach us to be humble and patient, and to remember that the Kingdom of God is righteousness and peace and joy in the Holy Ghost.
That we may continue a people to love and serve Thee.
That the men and women of our nation be sober, pure, and righteous ; brave to act, patient to bear, and earnest in obeying Thy will.

2. **The Queen and Royal Family.**
O God most high, Who art King of kings and Lord of lords.
replenish our queen with the grace of Thy Spirit, that she may always incline to Thy holy will :
endue her plenteously with heavenly gifts.

O God in whose hand are the hearts of kings.
govern our queen with Thy wisdom, that all her counsels may be pleasing in Thy sight :
grant her success in all that is good.

Preserve the Royal Family in the dangers and temptations of their high estate.

In all humility and godly fear, may they serve Thee faithfully, that they may inherit the crown of everlasting life.

3. **All rulers, statesmen, magistrates, and judges.**

O Lord, Who art the Counsellor, the mighty God, give them the spirit of wisdom and godly fear:

inspire them with the love of Christ and of men, that they may seek the enlightenment and welfare of all who are under their sway:

raise up for the service of our nation wise and faithful men who honour Thee:

that they may have grace to cast from them all self-seeking and unworthy ambition:

that they may be the defence of the oppressed, and the help of the orphan and the widow and the helpless.

4. **Parliament.**

O God Who art the fountain of all wisdom, guide our legislators.

Overrule their deliberations for the welfare of this great nation.

May the laws of our country reflect Thy will.

Prosper their counsels to the advancement of true religion, so that peace and happiness through Thy faith and fear may continue among us through all generations.

Give them as their end and aim the brotherhood of all men.

III.—Our City or Town, or Parish.

1. **The People.**
    May the least among us seek the honour of our town.
    May true religion spread among us, sobriety, &c.
    May all misery and vice and shame pass away.

2. **Magistrates.**
    May they as men of honour and uprightness consecrate their opportunities of serving men,
    > use their position for the raising of the fallen and the protection of the innocent:
    > strengthen the hands of the honest and upright:
    > destroy the power of deceit and greed and vice.

IV.—Classes.

1. **The poor.**
    O Lord Who has been a strength to the poor, a strength to the needy in his distress.
    > visit in Thy tenderness the needy in our infirmaries, and asylums, hospitals, poorhouses, and orphan homes.
    > Give tenderness to those that wait upon them.
    > Teach us to see in them thy brethren, and to pity and serve them.
    > May we learn to serve Thee in our service of them,
    >> visit the sick and the prisoner as those for whom Christ died,

minister unto the sorrowing and friendless as Thou hast ministered unto us.

2. **The rich.**
O God Who hast commanded us to lay up for ourselves treasures in heaven,
give to the rich grace to use their riches for Thy glory.
Make them good stewards of Thy bounty.
Keep far from them all pride, luxury, sloth.
Let them not be high-minded or neglectful of the poor.
Awaken in all the joy of blessing the needy.
Make them ready to give of their abundance for every noble work and Christian enterprise.

3. Grant grace to **all who are in high station**, all whose words are honoured, all whose example is imitated, that their words and their conduct may be wise and honourable:
that in nothing they may lead any to stumble or to doubt Thy truth, or dishonour Thy name.

4. **Working men and women.**
That they may be faithful and diligent, serving Thee:
that they may not be eye-servants.
Bless them in their callings and in their families.
May they use their great power in our nation for good—to establish the Kingdom of Heaven.

5. Give guidance to **all engaged in the lawful callings of life**,
> that all men may perform their duties as unto the Lord:
> that having gifts that differ, all may labour with one mind for one end.
> That all may rejoice with those that prosper, and be kind and helpful to those that fail.
> That in the struggle of life, we may all rejoice in hope, be patient in tribulation, and continue instant in prayer.

6. **Professors and teachers.**
> That they may be disciples of Thy wisdom, and obedient to Him who is the loving and wise Teacher of all.
> That their example may lead many to love what is noble, and to live for the honour of Thy name.
> Make them all seekers after truth, and with all their learning, may they know the fear and love of God.
> Enable them to train the rising generation for the service of God and of man.

7. **Men and women of influence.**
> Lead them by Thy light and truth.
> Make them obedient to that heavenly teaching of Thine.
> Guide those who are guiding our nation, and teach those who, by their words and writings, are forming public opinion.
> Give them a deep sense of their responsibility to Thee.

Fearing God, may they know no other fear.
May they be brave defenders of all that is true, pure, honourable, lovely, and of good report.

8. O Father, Who in Thy mercy hast never left us without **witnesses of Thy truth**.
raise up many who are full of faith and Thy Holy Spirit:
whose hearts are filled with the love of men:
who visit the fatherless and seek the lost:
who spend their days to dispel the darkness, and the sin of the world.
Grant them grace to persevere without wearying.
Give them strength to pray for those who resist their good work, and to rejoice when they are reviled and opposed in the service of truth.

V.—HOME.

1. **Our homes.**
O Father, Who in Thy lovingkindness hast set us in **families**,
teach us to realise the sacredness of home.
May every home among us be a nursery of piety and of noble youth.
May the influence of our home life be for God, and love and holiness.
May every home be a shelter from care and sin, a place where Thy Spirit rules.
May the memory of home follow the absent into far lands, chastening their hearts,

keeping them unspotted, and bringing them to Thee.

2. **The children.**
Give them love and reverence for their parents, that they may learn to love and reverence their Father in heaven.

Grant that they grow up into holiness, and strength, and fruitfulness, in all things just, true, and noble, before God and man.

Guard their purity and innocence; and when they learn what sin is, teach them to hate and fear it.

Keep them from the sins that have marred our lives.

May they find their happiness in seeking the happiness of each other.

May Thy Spirit Whose seal was set upon them in Baptism be with them always:
> confirming in them the love of all that is good and noble and fair:
> ripening in them the faith and love of Jesus Christ.

Satisfy them early with Thy mercy, that they may rejoice and be glad all their days.

Give them health and happiness.

Watch over them at school, in play, in temptation.

Put Thy hand upon them and bless them.

3. **Young men and women.**
Make them a joy to their parents, at home or absent.

Give them the grace of sobriety, purity, service.
Deepen their early piety and prayerfulness.
May they consecrate the freshness of their years and strength to God.
Be with them when they leave home: when surrounded by danger.
Keep those who are in our great cities when tempted.
Deliver those who are being led away by evil.
Give them all high conceptions of duty and the worth of life.
Suffer them not to forget the God of their fathers.
Give them grace to remember their aged fathers —widowed mothers—brothers and sisters.
May the prosperous never forget a struggling brother or sister.
Be with those in foreign lands.
Keep them in health and in holiness.

4. **All relatives and friends.**
Bless all who have been kind to us in past years:
who have helped, warned, encouraged us:
who have comforted us in our hours of sorrow:
who by their sympathy have given us hope:
who have patiently borne with our failings:
who have forgiven us our offences:
whose charity has covered our sins.

5. **The aged and infirm.**
O Eternal God, to Whom the years bring no change,
pity those whose strength is failing fast:

those going down the valley and are near the gate :
that, when the way seems dark, they may see beyond to the glorious light of Thy presence.
Be Thou their refuge and their support.
May they walk, leaning on Thy arm, and fearing no evil.
Grant that the closing years of their pilgrimage be spent in peace and the joy of Thy presence.

6. **The homeless, the poor and needy.**

O Lord Who hadst not where to lay Thy head, yet art now a shelter from the storm to all the weary,
take under thy protecting care all who are homeless :
who have no friend to succour them :
who have no human heart to pity them.
Give bread to the hungry.
Pity men and women who can find no work, and their children who are starving.
Pity the poor who are held down by adversity, and the weak who are baffled in struggle with the strong.
Find a home and tenderness for children who have been deserted by their parents.

7. **Our enemies.**

O Lord Who didst pray for Thy murderers,
give us grace to pray from the heart for those who hate us, wrong us, persecute us.

Bless those who hate us without cause :
who are estranged from us because we have reproved their sin :
who hinder thy work by thoughtless speech.
Take away all anger from them, and all bitterness from us.
Remove all misunderstandings and jealousies, and unite us to one another in increasing love.

VI.—Commerce, Business, and Social Life.

O God Who canst bring forth spiritual blessings out of all our conditions,
teach us both how to abound and to be in want.
Grant Thy presence to the prosperous that they may be humble :
and to those once prosperous that they complain not.
Take from us both the love of money and the fear of poverty.
Save us alike from courting the rich and despising the poor.
Give us grace to use all wealth and every talent as Thy stewards,
as those who must render an account to Thee :
to put out to usury for Thy glory even our poverty and our weakness.

O God Who wilt not be served deceitfully by any man,"
purify the politics of our nation :

calm the angry strife of men:
change bitterness of speech into charitable
    judgment:
make us with all our differences lovers of our
    country, and fellow-workers for its highest
    welfare.
Purify our social life, and grant
    that we may honour only that which is
    honourable:
deliver us from vanity, self-indulgence:
multiply the number of brave, earnest, self-
    sacrificing followers of Christ:
grant that we may encourage one another in
    pursuing all that is good.

O Lord, righteous and true, Whose cause and
    kingdom cannot be helped by evil,
purify our religious life from error and ignor-
    ance and self-will:
bring us nearer to the loving, holy life of Thy
    Son.

O God Who hast called Thy people to be the salt
    of the earth,
preserve us from those blemishes and failings
    that make the young and the ignorant to
    stumble:
grant us simplicity, truth, and fervour in our
    faith, and self-denial in our daily lives:
save us from all hypocrisy, insincerity, and
    formality.

VII.—THE CHURCH.

1. **The Church Universal, and our own branch of it.**
     O Lord Who hast loved the Church and given Thyself for it,
     sanctify and cleanse it by Thy Word.
     Where it is corrupt, purge; where in error, direct it.
     Where it is divided, heal the breaches thereof.
     Suffer not those whom thou hast redeemed with precious blood to be rent asunder.
     Make Thy strength perfect in our weakness.

     O Lord Who hast redeemed Thy Church that it should be holy and without blemish,
     remove all needless divisions, and unite us all in Thy holy work.
     Take away the spirit of rivalry, jealousy.
     Rebuke all our uncharitable judgments of one another.
     Teach us all to bear with one another where we differ, and to labour with one heart for the salvation of men.
     Bless all who love the Lord Jesus Christ by whatever name they are called.
     Guide them all into closer fellowship with Thee.
     Preserve Thy Church in unity and peace, free from persecution, or glorious under it.
     Keep her from trusting in the favour of princes, or the power of riches, or the ways of the world.
     Give her increasing trust in the power of

prayer and holiness, and the unfailing guidance of Thy spirit.
Grant that Christ may be more manifest in the lives of thy people,
and through their service and sacrifice work ever more powerfully upon the world.

2. **Our Congregation.**
O God Who givest grace unto every one of us according to the measure of the gift of Christ,
dwell with us and be our God.
Accept the worship we offer Thee this day.
Grant a blessing on all our efforts.
May Thy Spirit be the Teacher of all our classes.
May His presence be felt, and His voice heard in all our meetings:
Go Thou forth in Thy resistless might with those who work among the sinful, the degraded.
In all our work may we seek peace, giving place to one another, forbearing one another.
May each of us fear strife and covet the blessing of the peace-maker.

3. **Our office-bearers.**
O Thou Who art the wise and loving Shepherd, grant Thy Spirit to those who bear rule here in Thy name.
Give them the mind of the Good Shepherd, that they may faithfully and lovingly care for the flock.

Give us a sense of our responsibility to Thee, that we may be faithful stewards of Thy Word.
Grant zeal and wisdom and patience to all who plead for Thee :
    an unwavering faith in Thy promised victory over sin and death :
    bestow upon us all the Spirit of prayer.
Grant in mercy that our lives may commend the Lord Jesus Christ.
Give tender, loving hearts to understand the sorrows of men :
    courage and wisdom to speak the word in season.

4. **Our members and fellow-worshippers.**

Almighty God, who by Thy spirit helpest our infirmities,
enlighten those who are perplexed in faith.
Give peace in believing to those troubled in conscience.
To those who are tried in Spirit, give comfort.
Support those who are struggling against temptation.
Arouse the negligent, strengthen the penitent.
Deliver those who are in the bonds of sin, and are fighting for deliverance.
Give victory to those who are pressing toward Christ, who through all their failures and sins seek the perfect life of the Lord.
Grant the aid of Thy counsel to all who teach the ignorant and minister to the sick and sorrowing, who are seeking the lost, giving

hope to the despairing, and are encouraging those ready to faint.

May they know the blessedness of those who are fellow-workers with God.

5. **Mourners.**

O merciful and gracious Father, Who lovest whom Thou chastenest,

look down in pity upon those in sorrow.

Grant that, by the strength of Thy Spirit, they may not murmur in their hearts, but humbly submit unto Thy holy will.

Bless to them this hour of anguish, and make it the preparation for a life of greater nearness to Thee.

Lift up their hearts unto that home where there is no parting, and where Thou shalt wipe away all tears from their eyes.

In their darkness may thy light shine, and in their loneliness may Thy presence be felt.

The sorrows of death are but for a little while, comfort them with the living hope of a union that shall not be broken.

May we who remain behind a little longer keep ever clear and bright the memory of lives now passed into Thy presence.

As we try in our sorrow to follow them into the world unseen, grant that we may meet with Thee and know the comfort of Thy love.

6. **The sick, the burdened and friendless.**

O Father Who ever governest Thy children in mercy, look upon the sick with tender pity.

Sanctify Thy Fatherly correction.
May their weakness give strength to their faith and sincerity to their repentance.
Let Thy mercy encompass Thy afflicted children.
Make their affliction seem light and but for a moment compared with the eternal weight of glory hereafter.
Let the day of affliction be to them a holy messenger from Thee.
Forbid that their trials should lead them to doubt Thy care or Thy unceasing love of them.
Be the unfailing strength of those who are bearing crosses too heavy for them:
    whose sufferings make them weary for death:
    to whom the day brings no brightness and the night no rest:
    say to them, I will give thee rest:
    on whose hearts lie burdens none dare know but Thou:
    whose earthly future is without a ray of hope:
    who have lost their earthly friends and have not yet found Thee:
    who are in the snares of those who seek their ruin:
    over whom no one watches, for whom no one prays, whom no one seeks to save.

7. **The tempted and all who have gone astray.**
Visit in mercy speedily the sons and daughters of our home who are living in sin:

parents whose lives are leading their children astray:

grant that those who have known and yet have forgotten Thee may not perish but return to Thee again:

that those who follow Thee afar off may not deny Thee.

The outcasts of our cities.

In mercy rescue those

for whom the name of Christ is nothing but an oath.

O Father of the fatherless,

pity those who are trained by parents to a life of vice and crime.

who have known an earthly father's love and to whom Thy love is no more than a name.

Have mercy upon the great multitude of the Christless around our doors:

the criminals for whom we have done little, of whom we seldom think with tenderness:

the men and women abandoned by themselves and by us, that Thy spirit may never forsake them:

those who name the name of Christ, yet are too busy with the world for prayer:

who are ashamed to confess Thee.

who can be mocked and jeered into sin.

8. **The heathen—our missions.**

O God Who hast given Thy Son the heathen for His inheritance,

bless all who are labouring to bring them to Thee.
Give them the courage and wisdom of Christ: His patience and tenderness, His spirit of sacrifice.
As the fields ripen to the harvest, send forth labourers chosen by Thee.
More and more may Christ's Church take upon her heart the burden that lies on His.
Send forth many labourers in this great cause, feeling that it is Thine.
Gladden and sustain them till the promised day comes.

APPENDIX.

A Litany for Special Days of Prayer.

(from Hermann's "Consultation," slightly shortened and adapted.)

O God the Father of Heaven, O God the Son, Redeemer of the world, O God the Holy Ghost:
Have mercy upon us. Be gracious unto us, and spare us, good Lord.

From all sin, all error, and all evil:
Good Lord, deliver us.

From pestilence and famine, from lightning and tempests, from sedition and privy hatred, from murder and war, from dying an evil death suddenly and unprepared, from the snares of the devil, and from everlasting death:
Good Lord, deliver us.

By the mystery of Thy holy Incarnation; by Thy holy Nativity; by Thy Baptism, Fasting, and Temptations:
Good Lord, deliver us.

By Thine Agony and Bloody Sweat; by Thy Cross and Passion; by Thy Death and Burial; by Thy Resurrection and Ascension; by the Coming of the Holy Ghost, the Comforter:
Good Lord, deliver us.

In all time of our tribulation, in all time of our prosperity; in the hour of death, and in the Day of Judgment:
Good Lord, deliver us.

We sinners do beseech Thee to hear us, O Lord God; and that it may please Thee to rule and govern Thy holy Catholic Church in the right way:
We beseech Thee, hear us, good Lord.

That it may please Thee to keep all bishops, pastors, and ministers of Thy Church in wholesome doctrine and holy life, and to give unto all who hear increase of Thy Word and the fruit of Thy Spirit:
We beseech Thee, hear us, good Lord.

That it may please Thee to send forth faithful labourers into Thy harvest; to take away divisions and all offences; and to bring back into the way of truth all those that err and are deceived:
We beseech Thee, hear us, good Lord.

That it may please Thee to lift up them that be fallen, to strengthen them that stand, to comfort and help the weak-hearted and the tempted, and finally to tread down Satan under our feet:
We beseech Thee, hear us, good Lord.

That it may please Thee to give to all kings, rulers, and princes peace and concord; that Thou wilt graciously guide and keep our own [Queen] and all [her] Council-

lors; and that Thou wilt bless and guard our Magistrates and all our people:
We beseech Thee, hear us, good Lord.

That it may please Thee mercifully to look upon and save all that are in affliction and danger; all women in their time of peril; and that Thou wouldst cherish and care for all little children and sick folk:
We beseech Thee, hear us, good Lord.

That it may please Thee to give deliverance to prisoners, to defend and provide for all widows, and all fatherless and motherless children:
We beseech Thee, hear us, good Lord.

That it may please Thee to have mercy upon all men:
We beseech Thee, hear us, good Lord.

That it may please Thee to forgive our enemies, persecutors, and slanderers, and to turn their hearts:
We beseech Thee, hear us, good Lord.

That it may please Thee to give and preserve for us the fruits of the earth:
We beseech thee, hear us, good Lord.

O Lamb of God, who takest away the sins of the world, have mercy upon us. *Grant us Thy peace.*
Lord, have mercy upon us. *Christ, have mercy upon us.* Amen.

A Prayer after the Litany.

O God, from whom all holy desires, all right purposes, and all just works do proceed, grant unto Thy servants that peace which the world cannot give, that so our hearts being set on Thy precepts, and delivered from the fear of our enemies, we may live in peace and gladness under Thy Fatherly keeping, through our Lord Jesus Christ. Amen.

Section VI.

PRAYER FOR ILLUMINATION.

According to our standards and the teaching of the Reformed Church generally, the Word of God holds the first place among "the means of grace." The "preaching of the Word" is so important, and the responsibilities both of preacher and hearers are so great, that it is fitting and desirable that the sermon or lecture should have a brief prayer specially assigned to itself. This is commonly known as the "Prayer for Illumination," or for the special presence and power of the Holy Spirit with the Word. We strongly recommend that such prayer should be offered. Its place is, of course, immediately before the sermon. Specimens of what is meant are given.[1] A hymn, or part of one, containing petitions and aspirations for the Spirit, may sometimes take the place of this prayer, *e.g.*, "Come, Holy Ghost, our souls inspire"; "Spirit blest, who art adored"; "Holy Spirit, hear us."

I

Most Gracious God and Father, in whom dwelleth all fulness of light and wisdom: enlighten our minds, we beseech Thee, by Thy Holy Spirit, in the true understanding of Thy Word. Give us grace to receive it with

[1] The sources of some of these prayers are noted in Appendix.

all reverence and humility. May it teach us to put our whole trust in Thee only, and so to serve and honour Thee that in all our life we may glorify Thy Holy name and be profitable to our fellow-men. And inasmuch as it hath pleased Thee to number us with Thy servants and children, grant that we may render unto Thee the love and obedience which we owe Thee, as children to their Father, and servants to their lord. We ask all for the sake of Jesus Christ our only Saviour. Amen.

2

Mighty God, to whom all glory and honour do justly appertain: Since it hath pleased Thee to make us understand Thy will by Thy Holy Word, grant likewise that we may receive the same with all reverence, and that we may have a feeling of the force and strength thereof; that thereby we may be renewed unto all holiness of life; that in the end we may enjoy the heritage promised to all them that are adopted in Thy well-beloved Son, Jesus Christ our Lord. Amen.

3

O God, in whose wisdom Thy children become wise: Illumine our hearts by Thy Holy Spirit, that we may receive Thy truth in the love of it. May the fruit be unto holiness, and the end everlasting life, for the sake of Jesus Christ our Lord. Amen.

4

O God, who of old didst send forth Thy messengers to make rough places smooth and crooked paths straight, to prepare the way of the Lord: Prepare our hearts now to receive Thy Truth in the love of it. May the truth make us free from the bondage of error and evil with the glorious liberty of the children of God.

5

Almighty God, our heavenly Father, who hast given us Thy Holy Word to be a light to our feet and a lamp to our path : Grant us grace and faithfulness now to use it aright. Open our understandings and our hearts by Thy Holy Spirit that we may understand the Scriptures. Bless us in speaking and in hearing this day for Jesus' sake. Amen.

6

Almighty and everlasting God, who art the Father of lights : shine into our hearts and minds that we may understand aright Thy message to us in the Scriptures. Bless him who speaks and those who hear. May the Gospel come to us now, not in word only, but in power, and in the Holy Ghost. May He guide us into all truth, and strengthen us unto all obedience, so that we may be made meet to be partakers of the inheritance of the Saints in light, through Jesus Christ our Lord : To whom with Thee, and with the Holy Ghost, be all honour and glory, dominion and praise, now and for evermore. Amen.

7

O God, who didst speak of old unto the fathers by the prophets, and hast spoken unto us in these last days by Thy Son : speak to us now in Thy Holy Word. Make our hearts to be as good and prepared soil for the good seed of Thy Kingdom. Teach us to know Thy will and to do it in all things. May Thy Holy Spirit be with us now as a Spirit of light and life. May Christ be glorified in the preaching of His Gospel this day. And may grace and peace be multiplied unto us all through the knowledge of Thee and of Jesus our Lord: for His name's sake. Amen.

8

O Lord, as Thou feedest all creatures with temporal food and pasturage, make us to feel inwardly the effect of Thy holy Word; and grant that we, following Thy will declared therein, may in the end enjoy the heritage prepared for Thy people in Christ Jesus. Amen.

APPENDIX.

The first of the Prayers for Illumination given above is from Calvin; the second and eighth are from the Scottish Collects of 1595. Comp. Henry, *Leben Calvins* II., 156; *Beilage* 8, p. 65; Baird, *Chapter on Liturgies*, 37; Bannerman, *Worship of Presbyt. Church*, 101; *Presbyt. Forms of Service*, 2nd ed., 70.

Part II.

THE SACRAMENTS.

Section I.—BAPTISM.

A.—*BAPTISM OF INFANTS.*

The Sacrament of Baptism should, as far as possible, be administered in Church, and in presence of the Congregation.[1] It is an ordinance which concerns the whole Congregation, and not merely the child to be baptised and its parents; and ought, therefore, to be so administered as to be a means of grace to all present. The custom of requiring the father to stand up in presence of the Congregation during the address of the minister is not to be commended. It tends to convey the impression that the Congregation are mere spectators of a ceremony, and besides is largely responsible for the prevalent reluctance of parents to bring their children for public administration of the rite. Were the address directed to all the worshippers, although with special reference to parents, and the father asked to stand only when the baptismal vow was laid upon him, these evils might be greatly lessened.

[1] "Nor is it to be administered in private places or privately, but in the place of public worship, and in the face of the congregation, where the people may most conveniently see and hear" (Westminster Directory for Public Worship).

I.—Order of Baptismal Service.

1. Prayer.
2. Praise.
3. Passages from Scripture.
4. Address to the Congregation.
5. Prayer.
6. Baptism (all standing).
7. Anthem, "The Lord bless thee."
8. Prayer.

II.—Notes on Above Order.

1. Prayer invoking God's blessing upon all the worshippers in the administration of the Sacrament. This may form part of the prayer following the discourse.

2. A suitable Psalm, Hymn, or Anthem shall be sung, such as Ps. xc. 14-17, cxv. 12-18—"A little child the Saviour came"; "Blessed Jesus, here we stand"; "O Father, Thou who hast created all"; "Suffer the little children."

3. One or more passages of Scripture bearing on the Sacrament of Baptism may be read. These may form the subject of the Address. See Appendix I.

4. Exhortation: to be addressed to all the worshippers, to parents, to the young people on the significance of the Sacrament. See pp. 108-116.

5. The Baptismal Prayer: including Thanksgiving for the grace signified and sealed in the ordinance, along with supplication for a blessing on its administration.

6. As Baptism is the ordinance by which the Congregation solemnly recognises the child as a member of the Church, and receives it into Christian fellowship, it is

seemly that all should rise when the father rises to take the baptismal vow, and remain standing till after the singing of the Anthem.

The minister shall then put the following question to the father:[1] In presenting your child for Baptism, do you profess your faith in God the Father, Son, and Holy Ghost, and do you promise in dependence upon divine grace to train this child in the nurture and admonition of the Lord?

The answer of the father may be given either by bowing his head or by an audible "I do."

Sprinkling water on the child's face, the minister, naming the child, shall then say: "I baptise thee into the name of the Father, the Son, and the Holy Ghost," and may pronounce the apostolic benediction over him, "the grace of the Lord Jesus Christ, the love of God, and the communion of the Holy Ghost be with thee now and evermore. Amen."

The minister shall then turn to the Congregation and say: This child is now received into the fellowship of the Church of Christ. "Whoso," said the Lord, "shall receive one such little child in My name, receiveth Me."

7. The Congregation invoke God's blessing on the child in the words of the anthem: "The Lord bless thee and keep thee."

---

[1] The parents should be advised beforehand of the terms of this vow which they make on behalf of the child. Such a vow as is implied in the above question may be considered sufficient. In the Baptismal service in the Book of Common Order the father is called upon to repeat the Apostles' Creed, so as to "declare before God and His congregation the sum of that faith which ye believe, and wherein ye will instruct this child."

8. The Prayer after Baptism may include—

(*a*) *Thanksgiving* for the love of God in Christ to the children, and for the seal of this love in Baptism:

(*b*) *Prayer for the child* that God's fatherly love may shine upon his earthly path, that Christ may be his Redeemer and King, and that the Holy Spirit may dwell in him as his Teacher, Comforter, and Sanctifier: that he may be spared to be the joy of his parents and a strength to the Church, that grace may be given him to be a good soldier and faithful servant of Jesus Christ, and that he may at last attain an entrance into the heavenly kingdom:

(*c*) *Prayer for parents*, that their new joy may be sanctified, that grace may be given them for new responsibilities, that they may consecrate themselves afresh to God's service, and be baptized afresh with Christ's spirit of wisdom, faithfulness, and love:

(*d*) *Prayer for their home*, that Christ's presence may shed joy and peace abroad in it, that husband and wife, parents and children, brothers and sisters, may be drawn closer to each other in the bonds of divine love:

(*e*) *Prayer for all the homes of the congregation*, that the God of all the families of the earth would dwell in them; that he would sanctify and bless the ties of kinship; and that through His grace family discipline may serve to foster in all His children the spirit of trust, obedience, and love:

(*f*) *Prayer for the children of the congregation*, that they may be preserved from the evil that is in the world; may grow up in the Kingdom of God from the beginning; and may early be led into the conscious faith and willing service of Jesus Christ their Lord.

APPENDIX.

I.

Passages from Scripture.

(*See above, No. 3.*)

Go ye therefore and teach [make disciples of] all nations, baptizing them in [or into] the name of the Father, and of the Son, and of the Holy Ghost : teaching them to observe all things whatsoever I have commanded: and, lo, I am with you alway, even unto the end of the world. (Matthew xxviii. 19-20.)

And they brought young children to Him, that He should touch them : and His disciples rebuked those that brought them. But when Jesus saw it, He was much displeased, and said unto them, Suffer the little children to come unto Me, and forbid them not : for of such is the Kingdom of God. Verily I say unto you, whosoever shall not receive the Kingdom of God as a little child, he shall not enter therein. And He took them up in His arms, put His hands upon them, and blessed them. (Mark x. 13-16.)

Even so it is not the will of your Father which is in Heaven, that one of these little ones should perish. (Matt. xviii. 14.)

Take heed that ye despise not one of these little ones ; for I say unto you, that in heaven their angels do always behold the face of my Father which is in heaven. (Matt. xviii. 10.)

The promise is unto you, and to your children. . . . Ye are the children of the covenant which God made with our fathers, saying unto Abraham : And in thy seed shall all the kindreds of the earth be blessed. . . . That the blessing of Abraham might come on the Gentiles through Jesus Christ. . . . If ye be Christ's, then are ye Abraham's seed, and heirs according to the promise. . . . I will establish my covenant between me, thee and thy seed after thee in their generations, for an everlasting covenant, to be a God unto thee and to thy seed after thee. . . . It (circumcision) shall be a token of the covenant betwixt Me and you. (Gen. xvii. 7, 11 ; Acts ii. 39 ; iii. 25 ; Gal. iii. 29.) He is a Jew which is one inwardly; and circumcision is that of the heart, in the spirit, not in the letter. . . . The circumcision of Christ, buried with Him in baptism. (Rom. ii. 29 ; Col. ii. 11.)

The mercy of the Lord is from everlasting to everlasting upon them that fear Him, and His righteousness unto children's children ; to such as keep His covenant, and to those that remember His commandments to do them. (Ps. ciii. 17-18.)

John did baptize in the wilderness, and preach the baptism of repentance for the remission of sins. . . . And he preached, saying : There cometh one mightier than I after me, the latchet of whose shoes I am not worthy to stoop down and unloose. I indeed have baptized you with water: but He shall baptise you with the Holy Ghost. (Mark i. 4, 7-8.)

Know ye not, that so many of us as were baptized into Jesus Christ were baptized into His death ? Therefore we are buried with Him by baptism into death, that like as Christ was raised up from the dead by the glory of the Father, even so we also should walk in newness of life. (Rom. vi. 3-4.)

For ye are all the children of God by faith in Christ Jesus. For as many of you as have been baptized into Christ have put on Christ. (Gal. iii. 26-27.)

Then will I sprinkle clean water upon you, and ye shall be clean: from all your filthiness, and from all your idols, will I cleanse you. A new heart also will I give you, and a new spirit will I put within you : and I will take away the stony heart out of your flesh, and I will give you an heart of flesh. And I will put my spirit within you, and cause you to walk in my statutes, and ye shall keep my judgments, and do them. (Ezek. xxxvi. 25-27.)

And Hannah said: I am the woman that stood by thee here, praying unto the Lord. For this child I prayed; and the Lord hath given me my petition which I asked of him. Therefore also I have lent him to the Lord; as long as he liveth he shall be lent to the Lord. (1 Sam. i. 26-27.)

Thou shalt love the Lord thy God with all thy heart, and with all thy soul, and with all thy might. And these words, which I command thee this day, shall be in thine heart. And thou shalt teach them diligently unto thy children, and shalt talk of them when thou sittest in thine house, and when thou walkest by the way, and when thou liest down, and when thou risest up. (Deut. vi. 5.)

Ye fathers, provoke not your children to anger, lest they be discouraged. (Colossians iii. 21.)

Ye fathers, provoke not your children to wrath, but bring them up in the nurture and admonition of the Lord. (Ephesians vi. 4.)

II.
TOPICS FOR ADDRESS.[1]
(*See above, No. 4.*)

SIGNIFICANCE OF BAPTISM.

The sacraments as signs and seals of the covenant of grace—Baptism the initial sacrament of the Christian Church as circumcision of the Jewish one—The fundamental promise of the covenant in all ages is: "I will be a God unto thee and to thy seed after thee" (Gen. xvii. 7; comp. Rev. xxi. 3). "The blessing of Abraham," the Apostle teaches, "has come upon the Gentiles in Jesus Christ. . . . If ye be Christ's, ye are Abraham's seed, and heirs according to the promise." Therefore the children of believers, "born within the Church," as the Westminster Directory says, "have, by their birth, interest in the covenant, and right to the seal of it, and to the outward privileges of the Church, under the Gospel, no less than the children of Abraham in the time of the Old Testament; the covenant of grace, for substance, being the same, and the grace of God and the consolation of believers more plentiful than before. . . . Children, by baptism, are solemnly received into the bosom of the visible Church, distinguished from the world and them that are without, and united with believers. . . . They are federally 'holy' before baptism, and therefore are they baptized." (1 Cor. vii. 14.)

The Sacraments.—Christ's legacy to the Church—Comparison of Baptism with Lord's Supper—Baptism a

---

[1] Some of these may better be taken up in a Sermon on "The Children's Day," or other suitable occasion. The Address should be short and clear, and selection of topics made accordingly.

pledge of God's redeeming love, of the forgiveness of sin, of cleansing, and of new life through the Spirit.

The Great Name (Father, Son, and Holy Ghost) points to the spiritual heritage of baptized persons—God meeting the children on the threshold of their lives, and claiming to be their Father, their Redeemer, their Sanctifier.

The Work of the Spirit—Regeneration—Dying to sin, and living to God—The Symbolism of Baptism—The need of Spiritual Cleansing—Washing away the stains of the past, and emerging into a fresh, clean life—Putting on Christ.

Engagement to be the Lord's—Renouncing the world, the flesh, and the devil.

Children of Christian parents, members of the Christian Church, received by Baptism into the fellowship of the Church. "The inward grace and virtue of Baptism is not tied to that very moment of time wherein it is administered; but the fruit and power thereof reacheth to the whole course of our life." Children expected to grow up in the love and obedience of Christ—The duty of the Church towards the children.

The administration of the ordinance admonishes all that are present "to look back to their baptism, to repent of their sins against their covenant with God, to stir up their faith, to improve and make right use of their baptism, and of the covenant sealed thereby betwixt their souls and God."

Exhortation to Parents.

The Sacrament a comfort to Christian parents as a seal of the promise which is " unto them and unto their children."

Greatness of trust committed to their keeping—An immortal spirit to educate—Possibilities in a child—Hopes that centre in a child—Reverence for a child.

Baptism the solemn consecration of the child to God and to God's service—"I have lent him unto the Lord"—No magical efficacy in baptism—Efficacy bound up with religious training on the part of the parents—Consecration in baptism but the key-note of the whole training of the child—Fathers and mothers to consecrate their children daily.

Home training—The importance of *early* training—Children to be trained in obedience, reverence, and the love of Christ—Precept and example—Spirit of the home—Family religion—The power of home life—Its memories—Parents speaking to older children of the meaning of their baptism.

Personal consecration—The influence of children in the spiritual training of parents—Fresh dedication of the household to God—Need of divine help—Prayer.

Exhortation to the Young.

Baptized into the name of the Father—God's fatherly love—Christ's love for children—Stories in the Gospel. He called you by name in baptism; is calling you still. Have you answered to your name?

Dedicated to God in infancy your parents brought you—Samuel—Vow still resting upon you—The fulfilling of the vow—Engaged to be Christ's, and to fight against the world, the flesh, and the devil.

Enrolled in God's school—The teacher—The lessons.

Enlisted in God's army—The Captain of salvation—Enemies—Daily fight—Promise of victory.

III.
SPECIMEN FORMS OF PRAYER AND ADDRESS.
Prayer at Beginning of Baptismal Service.

Almighty and most merciful Father, who hast revealed Thy gracious purpose towards Thy children in Jesus Christ our Saviour, and who hast given us the sacraments of Thy Church as seals of Thy redeeming love, cleanse our hearts by the inspiration of Thy holy Spirit, that the administration of this ordinance may bring us a blessing, and quicken our faith, that we may lay hold of the grace set forth in the outward symbol for our growth in holiness, and to the praise of Thy great name, through Jesus Christ our Lord. Amen.

An Address to the Congregation.
(See above, No. 4.)

(Adapted from the Book of Common Order.)

This Baptism with water doth signify and set forth unto us the virtue of Christ's blood and righteousness, for cleansing our souls from the guilt and deadly poison of sin, that being born again of the Spirit we may walk in newness of life, of which grace Baptism is the covenant sign and seal.

Moreover, ye that be fathers and mothers may take from hence most singular comfort in seeing your children thus received into the bosom of Christ's Church; and by this also ye are daily admonished that ye bring up in piety and virtue these children of God's favour and mercy, over whom His fatherly providence watcheth continually.

Wherein if ye be negligent, ye shall not only do injury to your children, hiding from them the good pleasure of Almighty God their Father, but ye shall bring judgment upon yourselves, in suffering His children, bought with the blood of His dear Son, so traitorously, for lack of knowledge, to turn back from Him.

It much profiteth oft to be present at the administration of Baptism, that we being put in mind of the league and covenant made betwixt God and us,—that he will be our God and we His people, He our Father and we His children,—may have occasion to try our past lives as well as our present conduct, and to examine ourselves, whether we stand fast in the faith of God's elect, or contrariwise have strayed from Him through unbelief and ungodly living; whereof if our consciences do accuse us, yet by hearing the loving promises of our Heavenly Father (who calleth all men to mercy by repentance) we may from henceforth walk more warily in our vocation.

ANOTHER ADDRESS TO THE CONGREGATION AND TO THE PARENTS OF THE CHILD TO BE BAPTISED.[1]

1. Baptism, like the Lord's Supper, is a sign and seal of the covenant of grace. Every covenant which God made with men from the first had a sign as well as a word of promise connected with it, the sign making the

[1] There are occasions when it is desirable to give an address, such as this, indicating, rather more fully than usual, the nature and grounds of Infant Baptism. When that is done, the ordinary forenoon or evening service should be correspondingly shortened, so as to give due time for all connected with the Baptism, without any appearance of hurry, and without going beyond the usual limits of public worship.

word clearer and surer. And every covenant included the child with the parent. So it was in the covenant with Adam, with Noah, with Abraham, with Israel; and so with believers now under the Gospel.

"If ye are Christ's, then are ye Abraham's seed, and heirs according to the promise." Listen to it: "I will establish My covenant between Me and thee, and thy seed after thee in their generations for an everlasting covenant, to be a God unto thee and to thy seed after thee." In baptism, as now administered, "the promise" comes "to you and to your children" both in word and sign. God says to you to-day, as of old to Abraham, "the father of all them that believe": "This is the token of the covenant between Me and thee and thy seed after thee." He is "a gracious God and merciful." He thinks still of all the little ones "who cannot discern between their right hand and their left." But He has a special love and care for the children of His believing people. This is a perpetual witness in His Church that it is so.

See, then, that you have an interest in the covenant. Take hold afresh of Christ, in whom all its promises have their yea and amen, as you seek the sign of the covenant now for your child, or as you remember how you brought your little ones for baptism, as our brother brings his to-day. This is a *believer's* privilege. It is on the ground of a profession of faith in Christ and obedience to Him that I administer this sacrament to-day. The covenant promises and blessings are sure as the faithfulness of God, if there is faith on our part to lay hold of them. It is a *disciple's* ordinance, a token from the Lord's own hand of His love for you and yours. Remember a *disciple* means one who has come into the school of Christ, and is willing to learn of Him and to follow Him in all things.

2. Baptism shews the kind of blessing needed by our children from the first, and provided for them in God's covenant of grace and peace. It is "a visible sermon" on sin and cleansing and consecration. It teaches us that we are born with sinful natures,—a sad inheritance from fathers and mothers, themselves sinful; that even such little ones as these need, in God's sight, to be washed and purified. And it points to the great Divine remedy, to the blood of Christ and the power of the Holy Spirit. The Lord Jesus speaks to us by the signs of His sacrament to-day, saying: "Ye must be born again . . . born of water and of the Spirit." . . . "In Him we have redemption through His blood, the forgiveness of sins." Among the promises of the new covenant these stand chief: "Then will I sprinkle clean water upon you, and ye shall be clean, from all your filthiness will I cleanse you. A new heart also will I give you, and a new spirit will I put within you. I will put My spirit within you, and cause you to walk in My statutes and do them. . . . And ye shall be my people, and I will be your God."[1] As parents present their little ones for baptism in God's house—making this their first public act with respect to them—they profess anew their faith in these great foundation truths of the Gospel. They seek these covenant blessings for themselves and their children. The signs repeat the words to us to-day. They seal the promises to faith.

3. The Lord meets you, fathers and mothers, now with a very gracious message, and with His hands full of

---

[1] John iii. 5-7; Eph. i. 7; Ezek. xxxvi. 25-28.

gifts. It is at His invitation that you bring your little ones to Him in His house, as of old the earthly parents of the Holy Child Jesus brought Him, as an infant, to the Temple to present Him to the Lord. There is a special blessing prepared for you also as you do this, in the midst of His worshipping people, who join with you in prayer that all covenant promises may be fulfilled for you and your children. The Lord himself is here to meet with you and them for good. He bids you now cast all your cares for them upon Him, for He careth for them.

"They brought their babes unto Jesus that he would touch them. . . . "And He took them up in His arms, put His hands upon them, and blessed them."[1] We cannot see His look and gesture now as those mothers did, but surely faith may see in this ordinance the Lord's hand stretched out once more to receive and bless the little ones thus brought to Him for blessing, and may hear His voice saying to each believing father and mother: "According to thy faith be it unto thee. Take this child and train it for Me, and I will give thee thy wages."

In Baptism the Lord gives to the children of His people a place and a name in the fellowship of His Church on earth, a right to all its privileges, so far as their age allows, a claim to Christian instruction and loving Christian oversight. He gives these little ones [this little one] to-day a special right to our prayers on their [his] behalf both now and henceforth. We see the Good Shepherd now putting His mark on these lambs of the flock. They are specially dear to Him, and should

---

[1] Luke xviii. 15; Mark x. 16.

be so to us also. Let us see that we shew it more and more in this congregation. In token of our receiving and welcoming these little ones to-day, let us all rise now and remain standing during the administration of the ordinance.[1]

4. Encouraged by such tokens for good from the Lord in His house to-day, you, the father [and mother] of this little one, take upon you all the duties of Christian parents. The charge which Christ once gave to an apostle He gives now to you: "Feed my lambs." Ask the food from the Lord Himself. "Suffer these little children to come unto Him, and forbid them not." See that there is nothing in yourselves, or in your home life, to keep the little ones from coming to the Lord Jesus, but everything to help and encourage them to come. Remember the duties of "the Church in the house." Train up your children in the knowledge of God's Word, and especially of the great truths of the Gospel. Bring them afresh to the Lord day by day in prayer, lead them in His ways by example and counsel. Seek that, from the first, there may be always around them the pure and healthful atmosphere of a Christian home, where there is God's fear and God's love, and the blessing promised to the families that call upon His name.

These truths concerning God the Father, the Son, and the Spirit, and the way of salvation by Jesus Christ, you believe; and these duties, God helping you, you desire and purpose to perform,—do you not?

[The answer may be given either by bowing reverently, or by an audible "I do."]

---

[1] The parents should, of course, rise also at this point, and this should be explained to them beforehand. See above, p. 103.

Baptismal Prayer.

(See above, No. 5.)

(Adapted from the Book of Common Order.)

Almighty and everlasting God, who of Thine infinite mercy and goodness hast promised unto us that Thou wilt be not only our God, but the God and Father of our children, we beseech Thee to sanctify with thy Spirit and to receive into the number of Thy children this infant, whom we are now to baptise according to Thy word. Grant that he, coming to mature age, may confess Thee the only true God, and Jesus Christ whom Thou hast sent, and may serve Thee and be profitable unto Thy Church all the days of his life. And when this life is ended may he be brought unto the full fruition of Thy joys in the heavens, where Thy son, our Saviour Christ, reigneth with Thee the Father and with the Holy Ghost, world without end. Amen.

Baptismal Prayer.

(Adapted from the Directory for Public Worship.)

O God, who hast not left us as strangers without the covenant of promise, graciously vouchsafe to sanctify and bless this ordinance. Be pleased, we beseech Thee, to join the inward baptism of the Spirit with the outward baptism of water. Make this baptism to this child a seal of adoption, remission of sin, regeneration and eternal life, and all other promises of the covenant of grace. May he be planted into the likeness of the death and resurrection of Christ, and the body of sin being destroyed in him, may he serve Thee in newness of life all his days, through Jesus Christ our Lord. Amen.

Prayer after Baptism.

(Adapted from the Book of Common Order.)

Most holy and merciful Father, we give Thee most humble thanks for Thine infinite goodness, who has not only numbered us amongst Thy Saints, but also of Thy free mercy dost call our children unto Thee, marking them with this Sacrament as a singular token and badge of Thy love. Wherefore, most loving Father, we beseech Thee, for Christ's sake, that Thou wilt confirm this Thy favour more and more towards us, and take into Thy tuition and defence this infant whom we offer and present unto Thee with common supplications. Suffer him not so to fall away from Thee, as to lose the force of his baptism, but through the Holy Spirit working in his heart may he know Thee His merciful Father, and prevail against Satan, that in the end he may obtain the victory and be exalted into the freedom of Thy Kingdom. Amen.

B.—*BAPTISM OF ADULTS.*

As in the Jewish Church in our Lord's time, and for centuries previous, the circumcision of infants was the rule and that of adults the exception, so in our own Church, save in its mission fields, the Baptism of Adults is of comparatively rare occurrence. It is the more desirable, accordingly, that all due care be taken to render the observance of it as impressive and edifying as possible. The Catechumen must be duly instructed as to the meaning of the faith of which he is to make profession, and the nature of the obligations it lays upon him. When practicable, the ordinance should be celebrated in presence of the Congregation; the whole service should culminate in its celebration; and generally, as in the administration of Infant Baptism, every means should be used to lead all to realise afresh the gracious privileges and responsibilities it carries with it.

I.—Order of Baptismal Service.

1. Prayer.
2. Psalm or Hymn.
3. Passages from Scripture.
4. Address to the Congregation.
5. Address to the person to be baptized.
6. Profession of faith on the part of the person to be baptized.
7. Baptismal Prayer.
8. Baptism.
9. Anthem, "The Lord bless thee," &c.
10. Post-baptismal Prayer.
11. Charge to the newly-baptized person.

II.—Notes on the above Order.

1. Prayer at beginning of Service, as in order of Infant Baptism.

2. Psalm or Hymn. Psalms li.; cxvi. 1-8; cxix. 1-8, 57-60. Hymns, "O for a heart to praise;" "Come, Holy Spirit;" "O Jesus, I have promised;" "Jesus, Master, whose I am;" "Fight the good fight;" "Soldiers of Christ, arise;" "O happy day that fixed my choice."

3. Passages from Scripture to be read.

Go ye and teach all nations, baptizing them in the name of the Father, and of the Son, and of the Holy Ghost; teaching them to observe all things whatsoever I have commanded you; and, lo, I am with you alway, even unto the end of the world. (Matt. xxviii. 19, 20.)

John did baptize in the wilderness, and preach the baptism of repentance for the remission of sins. . . . And he preached, saying, There cometh one mightier than I after me, the latchet of whose shoes I am not worthy to stoop down and unloose. I indeed have baptized you with water; but He shall baptize you with the Holy Ghost. (Mark i. 4, 7, 8.)

Know ye not, that so many of you as were baptized into Jesus Christ were baptized into His death? Therefore we are buried with Him by baptism into death; that like as Christ was raised up from the dead by the glory of the Father, even so we also should walk in newness of life. (Rom. vi. 3, 4.)

For ye are all the children of God by faith in Christ Jesus. For as many of you as have been baptized into Christ have put on Christ. (Gal. iii. 26, 27.)

Then will I sprinkle clean water upon you, and ye shall be clean; from all your filthiness, and from all your idols, will I cleanse you. A new heart also will I give you, and a new spirit will I put within you; and I will take away the stony heart out of your flesh, and I will give you an heart of flesh. And I will put my Spirit within you, and cause you to walk in my statutes, and ye shall keep my judgments, and do them. . . . And ye shall be My people, and I will be your God. (Ezek. xxxvi. 25-28.)

4. Address to the Congregation.

Topics for Address, as in order of Infant Baptism, omitting what refers to children.

The administration of this ordinance should remind all who are present that "the needful but much neglected duty of improving our baptism is to be performed by us all our life long, especially in the time of temptation, and when we are present at the administration of it to others: by serious and thankful consideration of the nature of it, and of the ends for which Christ instituted it, the privileges and benefits conferred and sealed thereby, and our solemn vow made therein; by being humbled for our sinful defilement, our falling short of, and walking contrary to, the grace of baptism, and our engagement; by growing up to assurance of pardon of sin, and of all other blessings sealed to us in that sacrament; by drawing strength from the death and resurrection of Christ, into whom we are baptized, for the mortifying of sin, and quickening of grace; and by endeavouring to live by faith, to have our conversation in holiness and righteousness, as those that have therein given up their names to Christ; and to walk in brotherly love, as being baptized by the same spirit into one body." (Larger Catechism, Q. 167.)

5. Address to the person to be baptized.

You are about to be baptized, according to the ordinance of Christ, into the name of the Father and of the Son and of the Holy Ghost. This implies that you solemnly dedicate yourself to the loving service of the God into whose name you are baptized, the one living and true God, Father, Son, and Holy Ghost, taking the Father to be your Father, the Son to be your Saviour and Lord, the Holy Ghost to be your Sanctifier and Comforter.

And while you thus dedicate yourself to the Lord, He conveys to you by means of this ordinance the gladdening assurance that the blessings which the water of baptism represents are freely given to you. He invites you to rejoice in the assurance that the blood of Jesus Christ His Son cleanseth you from all sin, and that the Spirit of Christ is given to you to renew you in holiness, to fit you for the work and warfare to which you are called, and to make you meet for the inheritance of the saints in glory.

6. The adult to be baptized should then be asked to make solemn profession of his faith and of his engagement to be the Lord's.

The profession of faith may be made in such terms as those of the Apostles' Creed, the minister asking the person to be baptized:

"Do you believe in God the Father Almighty?" &c. Or, more briefly:

Do you desire, by receiving Christian baptism, to make public profession of your faith in the Lord Jesus Christ as your Saviour, and of your devotion to Him as your Divine Master and Lord.

Do you promise and engage, in humble dependence upon Divine grace, to live as a faithful servant of the Lord Jesus Christ, seeking to adorn the doctrine of God your Saviour in all things, and to show forth in your life the praises of Him who hath called you out of darkness into His marvellous light?

7. Baptismal prayer.

Almighty God, the Father of our Lord Jesus Christ, who hast called us to be partakers of Thy great mercy in the fellowship of faith, and hast appointed this ordinance of baptism to be a precious means of grace to Thy believing people, graciously vouchsafe to bless this ordinance to him who is about to be baptized. Be pleased, we beseech Thee, to join the inward baptism of the Spirit with the outward baptism of water. Make this baptism unto him a seal of adoption, remission of sin, regeneration and eternal life. And grant, most merciful Father, that being conformed to Thy Son in His death and resurrection, he may walk before Thee in newness of life all his days, through Jesus Christ our Lord.

8. Baptism.

Sprinkling water on the head of Catechumen (who kneels) the minister, naming him (or her) shall say: "I baptize thee into the name of the Father, the Son, and the Holy Ghost," adding either the words: "The very God of peace sanctify thee wholly; and I pray God thy whole spirit, and soul, and body be preserved blameless unto the coming of our Lord Jesus Christ;" or the Apostolic Benediction: "The grace of the Lord Jesus Christ," &c.

The Minister shall then turn to the Congregation and say: "Our brother (or sister) is now received into the fellowship of the Church of Christ. Wherefore receive ye one another as Christ also received us, to the glory of God."

9. The Congregation invoke God's blessing in the words of the anthem: "The Lord bless thee," &c.

10. Post-baptismal Prayer.

Almighty and ever-blessed God, we render unto Thee most humble and hearty thanks for Thy great goodness in giving us a place within Thy Church and marking us with the seal of Thy love in this ordinance of Baptism.

We pray for him who has now been baptized, that Thy fatherly love may shine upon his earthly path, that the grace of the Lord Jesus Christ may make him strong for the work and warfare to which he is called, and that the blessed Spirit of all grace may dwell within him as his Guide and Teacher, his Comforter and Sanctifier. May he have grace given him to be faithful to the engagements into which he has entered, and to live as befits one who has been called unto Thy Kingdom and glory and who has solemnly dedicated himself unto Thee. Strengthened by Thy Spirit in the inner man, may he fight the good fight of faith, and endure unto the end, and have an entrance ministered to him abundantly into Thy heavenly kingdom, through Jesus Christ our Lord, unto whom, with Thee and the Holy Ghost, be honour and glory everlasting. Amen.

11. Brief charge to the newly baptized person, urging to fidelity to the Master Whose name he now bears, to the Kingdom in which he is a member, and to the body of the faithful with whom he is united in Jesus Christ.

Section II.

THE LORD'S SUPPER, OR THE COMMUNION.

I.—Preparation.

1. As the Westminster Directory recommends, on the Lord's Day before that on which the Communion is to be administered, "something concerning the Ordinance, and the due preparation thereunto, and participation thereof, should be taught: that by the diligent use of all means, public and private, all may come better

prepared to that heavenly Feast." One may generally count upon a very full attendance of the congregation on that Sabbath. For the "Fencing," in several aspects of it, this is a specially suitable time.

2. Where the old Sacramental Fast-day has disappeared, one or more Preparation Services should be held towards the end of the week. Friday evening and Saturday afternoon are usually found specially suitable for this purpose. At one or other of these Services, or on the Sabbath evening preceding, the Young Communicants should be received and welcomed to the Fellowship of the congregation in name of the Kirk-Session. Care should be taken to have the subjects of sermon or address, the prayers, psalms, and hymns, in keeping with the objects of a season of "recollection" and self-examination before the Communion.

II.—COMMUNION SABBATH SERVICES.

Special pains should be given to have the whole of the praise, prayers, Scripture readings, and sermon in harmony with the spirit of a Communion time as a Christian festival, a time of special religious privilege and gladness. Such psalms and hymns may be used as

Psalm xliii. 3-5—"O send Thy light forth."
,, xxiii.—"The Lord 's my Shepherd."
,, xlv. 2-8—"Thou fairer art than sons of men."
,, xcvi. or xcviii.—"O sing a new song to the Lord."
,, c.—"All people that on earth do dwell."
,, ciii.—"O thou my soul, bless God the Lord."
,, cvi.—"Give praise and thanks unto the Lord.
,, cvii.—"Praise God for He is good."

Psalm cxvi.—"I love the Lord, because my voice."
,, cxvi. 13-19—"I'll of salvation take the cup."
,, cxviii. 19-29—"O set ye open unto me."
,, cxxii.—"I joyed when to the House of God."
,, cxxxii. 13-18—"For God of Zion hath made choice."
,, cxxxvi., 1st or 2nd version.
,, cxlv., 2nd version, 9-16—"Good unto all men is the Lord."

Hymns:—
"According to Thy gracious word."
"'Twas on that night."
"By Christ redeemed."
"Here, O my Lord."
"Jesus, Thou joy of loving hearts."
"Sit down beneath His shadow."
"Till He come—O let the words."

Such themes are in season as the glory of Christ in His Person and Work, the Atonement, the Resurrection, the Ascension, the Second Coming, and the glory of the inheritance of the saints in Christ here and hereafter, the privileges and possibilities of the Christian life. Action Sermons and Table Addresses may be founded on such passages of Scripture as those which describe the marriage union of Christ and His Church, our Lord's last words to His disciples in the Gospel of St John, the prayers and doxologies in the Pauline Epistles, the songs of heaven in the Book of the Revelation.

"The dispensation of the Sacrament" should, as a rule, follow closely upon "the dispensation of the Word," as a "seal" to the gospel preached. The old custom of three Table Services following the Action

Sermon was open to some objections, but was strong in respect of the continuity of the impression made. The plan which best preserves this advantage, besides having other recommendations, is that of "simultaneous Communion." The method of having an ordinary forenoon service, followed by an interval of considerable length and an afternoon Communion service, involves the loss of continuity of impression and other practical disadvantages. If an interval is felt desirable to allow members of the same family to communicate on the same Sabbath without inconvenience (although experience shows that the difficulty supposed to exist in this direction may easily be exaggerated), the best plan is to make the interval not too long, and either to conduct the afternoon service as a "Second Table" in continuation of the forenoon Communion service, the consecration prayer being referred to as already offered, or to repeat the warrant for the ordinance and the consecration prayer, if the communicants at the Second Table were not for the most part present in the forenoon. In this case, while the Assistant Minister takes the Second Table, the Minister of the congregation may with advantage take the concluding prayer.

There ought to be thought and consultation with the Elders beforehand as to all arrangements bearing on the order and seemliness of the whole service. Changes even in what may seem trifling details should not be hastily made. Tender and sacred associations gather for the worshippers round every part of the Communion Services. The 103rd Psalm and the 35th Paraphrase, for example, have a quite peculiar power from their use at Communion seasons in Scotland from generation to generation. Many do not realise—to give another illustration—how impressive, especially to young people and children, is the effect of the "fine linen, clean and white," covering not the Table before the Minister only, but all the Tables where the communicants sit. It is very desirable that this simple ceremonial, all the more impressive because of its rarity in the worship of the Reformed Church, should not be abolished. In some instances, in which this old custom, after being disused for a time, was restored, Ministers and Elders have been surprised at the warmth of approval with which the restoration was hailed by some of the most devout and intelligent worshippers in the congregation.

The Act of Assembly, 1645[1] "ordains that," besides the Action Sermon, "there be a Sermon of Thanksgiving after the Communion is ended." The "Monday Thanksgiving Service" has associations with John Livingstone's sermon at the Kirk of Shotts, on a Monday after the Communion there in 1630, and with other times of special blessing. Where there is no such service on the following day, it is the more desirable that the element of thanksgiving, along with practical directions and exhortations bearing on the Christian life, should have a prominent place in the service of the Communion Sabbath evening.

III.—Outline of Order of Communion.

1. Words of Institution read.
2. Fencing.
3 Psalm or Hymn.
4. Thanksgiving and Consecration Prayer.
5. [Short Table Address. Optional, may precede 4.]

[1] See note *infra*, p. 131.

6. Distribution of elements, with our Lord's words repeated.
7. Short Table Address.
8. Psalm ciii.
9. Closing Prayer.
10. Psalm, Hymn, or Doxology.
11. Benediction.

IV —Notes on above Order.

After the Action Sermon and singing of a psalm or hymn,[1] the Minister continuing in the pulpit :[2]

1. **Words of Institution read**, as our warrant for the Ordinance, from 1 Cor. xi. 23-32, or the Gospels.

2. **Fencing**, or "**Exhortation, Warning, and Invitation**" [Westminster Directory]. These three elements, however briefly, should enter into this part of the service. See the specimen forms given in Appendix, pp. 133-139.

3. **Psalm**, or **Paraph.** xxxv. : " 'Twas on that night."
Elements brought forward and placed on the Table. Minister and Elders take their places there.[3]

---

[1] In the service of the Book of Common Order in Knox's time, as in Calvin's Order of Geneva, the "Apostles' Creed" was rehearsed at the end of the prayer after sermon. This might well form part of our Communion Service, where found for edification. The Lord's Prayer should also come in at an earlier part of the morning service.

[2] So both in the Book of Common Order and the Directory until *after the Fencing*. The former puts the words of Institution *before* the Fencing ; the latter makes them the first words *after* it, "the Minister being now at the Table."

[3] Where there are two Table Services with an interval, the Minister who presides, and the Elders who serve, at the first Table, communicate at the second. Where there is simultaneous Com-

4. **Thanksgiving and Consecration Prayer.**
This should, as a rule, embrace the following elements—

(1) Adoration and confession of sin (briefly).
(2) Thanksgiving, especially for redemption, the sacrifice of Christ, the Church and means of grace, the Lord's Supper, the fellowship of saints on earth and in heaven.
(3) Prayer for special access and blessing in the Sacrament, for the presence of the Father, Son, and Spirit, for sanctification of the elements, for faith to receive Christ now in His ordinance, for living union and fellowship with Him.
(4) Offering and consecration of ourselves to God in Christ.
(5) Doxology.

See specimen forms given in Appendix, pp. 140-143.

5. **Short Table Address** [Optional—may be given *before* the Thanksgiving and Consecration Prayer, if preferred]. A few words may offer themselves naturally from the subject of sermon with special application to the Ordinance. As has been suggested, our Lord's own directions for right communicating may be helpful. (1.)

munion one or other of two plans may be followed :—(1.) The Minister gives the Bread and Wine to an Elder seated on each side of him. They partake and give back the elements to him. He partakes, and after a short pause gives the Bread and the Cup to the rest of the Elders, who serve the communicants, return with the elements to the Table before the Minister, and take their seats there. The two Elders, who first partook, then rise, and serve their brethren. (2.) The Minister gives the Bread and Wine to the Elders seated round the Table at which he stands. The elements pass round the Elders and return to the Minister, who receives them from one of the Elders and partakes himself. Then, after a short pause, the Elders rise and serve the rest of the communicants.

"Remember Me." (2.) "Take" what He offers to us here and now in Himself. (3.) "Eat." Feed on Him by faith for the supply of all spiritual needs. (4.) "Drink." Receive all covenant blessings, the wine of refreshment and gladness in His Kingdom. (5.) "This do." Mode and results of appropriating Christ. The union a vital one. "Quis separabit?" The first and last of these might suitably form subject of Post-Communion address.

6. **Distribution of the elements,** with the words: "The Lord Jesus, the same night in which He was betrayed, took bread: and when He had given thanks He brake it, and said, Take, eat; this is My body which is broken for you: this do in remembrance of Me. After the same manner also He took the cup, when He had supped, saying, This cup is the new covenant in My blood: this do, as oft as ye drink it, in remembrance of Me." [The Minister should add the words of the Apostle]: "For as often as ye eat this bread and drink this cup, ye do shew the Lord's death till He come." Thereafter there should, as a rule, be silence at the Table, until all have partaken.[1]

---

[1] This was the judgment of the General Assembly of 1645, in an important Act which is "virtually an Appendix to the Directory," in which they "approve of the opinion of their committee . . . in some points of public worship." See Sprott and Leishman's ed. of Book of Common Order and Directory, p. 267, also Acts of General Assembly (Church Law Society ed.), p. 120. "That there be silence during the time of the Communicants' receiving," seems to be laid down as the general rule, qualified by a certain discretion given to the Minister, "except only when he expresseth some few short sentences, suitable to the present condition of the communicants . . . that they may be incited and quickened in their meditations in the Action."

7. **Short Table Address.** [This should be chiefly of a practical sort, bearing on Christian life and service. "The Directions"—to use the suggestive name which this address received in olden days of the Scottish Church—may be drawn from such passages as Rom. xii.; Eph. iv. 1-5, v. 1-20; Phil. ii. 1-8, iv. 1-9; Col. iii. 1-17; Titus ii. 11-14; Heb. x. 23-25, xii. 11, xiii. 20 *f.*; 1 Peter ii. 1-5; 2 Peter i. 3.]

8. **Psalm 103**: "O thou my soul, bless God the Lord."[1]

9. **Closing Prayer.**—(1.) Thanksgiving for blessing received, and prayer for the communicants, and all the congregation, especially the children and young people present. (2.) Prayer for our own Church, and for the Catholic Church of Christ, militant here on earth. (3.) Thanksgiving for the Church triumphant, and prayer for the coming and kingdom of our Lord Jesus Christ.[2] [Comp. Appendix, pp. 143-145, and Euchologion, 6th ed., p. 299-302, for *selection*.]

10. **Closing Psalm, Hymn, or Doxology.**

11. **Benediction.**—Heb. xiii. 20 *f.*, with Apostolic benediction.

---

[1] This is the psalm especially recommended for use when "the Action is ended" in Knox's Book of Common Order. It has held its place in Scotland for nearly three centuries and a half.

[2] Topics (2) and (3) are introduced at this point in the "Westminster Directory" as revised by Committee of Presbyterian Church of England in 1892; so also in the "Order for the Celebration of the Communion," used in St Giles', Edinburgh (2nd ed., p. 168), and in the "Order for Administration of the Lord's Supper in Presbyterian Forms of Service," issued by the "Devotional Service Association" of the United Presbyterian Church (2nd ed., p. 106), and in Euchologion as above.

APPENDIX

Consisting of the Specimen Forms to which reference is made above.

I.—Fencing or Exhortation before the Communion.

(From Book of Common Order, revised and shortened.)

Dearly Beloved in the Lord, as we are now met to keep this ordinance of Christ, let us consider these words of the Apostle spoken concerning it, and how he exhorteth us to examine ourselves before we eat of this bread and drink of this cup. For as the benefit is great if with true, penitent, and believing hearts we receive this holy sacrament, so is the danger great if we receive the same unworthily.

Therefore, in the name and authority of God, and of His Son Jesus Christ, I forbid from this Table all blasphemers of God, all unclean and intemperate persons, all who cherish anger or envy against their fellows, or who live a life directly fighting against the will and commandment of God, charging them, as they will answer in the presence of Him who is the righteous Judge, that they presume not to profane this holy Table. And yet this I pronounce not to seclude any penitent person, how grievous soever his sins before have been, if so be that he feel in his heart repentance for the same, and hath turned from them, but only such as continue in sin without repentance.

Neither are they excluded, but rather are they encouraged to come, who long after a greater perfection than they can in this present life attain unto. For albeit we feel in ourselves much frailty and wretchedness, in that our faith oftentimes faileth, and we rebel and murmur against God's will toward us, and have need daily to fight against the lusts of our flesh; yet seeing that our Lord hath printed His Gospel in our hearts, so that we are kept from falling into despair and unbelief, seeing also that He hath given us some desire to withstand our own evil affections and some longing after holiness, we may now be right well assured that our sins and manifold shortcomings shall not hinder Him from accepting us as worthy to come to His Table. For the end of our coming thither is not to make protestation that we are upright or pure in our lives; but contrariwise, we come to seek our life and perfection in Jesus Christ.

Let us consider, then, that this Sacrament is a singular medicine for all poor sick creatures, a comfortable help to weak souls, and that our Lord requireth no other worthiness on our part, but that we unfeignedly acknowledge our need of His healing and strengthening, and do truly cast ourselves upon Him.

Let us then render all praise, thanks, and glory unto God the Father, that it hath pleased Him to grant unto us sinners so excellent a gift and treasure as to receive us by His Spirit into the fellowship of His dear Son, Jesus Christ our Lord, whom He delivered unto death for us, and giveth Him also unto us now as our necessary food and nourishment unto everlasting life. And let us lift up our minds and hearts now by faith unto the Lord who hath said, "This do ye in remembrance of Me;" saying also unto all them that obey

Him, "Lo, I am with you alway, even unto the end of the world." Amen.

II.—EXHORTATION, WARNING, and INVITATION, from Westminster Directory.

(Revised, chiefly as by Committee of English Presbyterian Synod in 1892.)

Dear Brethren, it is meet that those who purpose to come to the Lord's Table should consider the meaning and ends of this Sacrament, wherein Christ and all the blessings of the new Covenant are set forth and sealed to believers, and the great necessity of having our comforts and strength renewed thereby in this our pilgrimage and warfare. And as the benefit is great, if we come to this Table with knowledge, faith, repentance, love, and purpose of new obedience, and with souls hungering and thirsting after Christ: so also is the danger great, if we eat and drink unworthily.

Therefore, in the name of Christ, I do, on the one part, warn all such as are scandalous and profane, or that live in any sin against their conscience, that they presume not to come to this holy Table, inasmuch as he that eateth and drinketh unworthily, eateth and drinketh judgment to himself. But, on the other part, I do in an especial manner invite and encourage all who labour under a sense of the burden and defilement of their sins, and who desire to reach out unto a greater progress in grace than they have yet attained unto, to come to the Lord's Table, assuring them in His name of welcome, and of refreshment and strength to their weak and wearied souls.

III.

Instead of Fencing the Tables, a selection from the following passages of Scripture may be read:—

1. The Ten Commandments:—

"And God spake all these words, saying: I am the Lord thy God, which have brought thee out of the land of Egypt, out of the house of bondage. Thou shalt have no other gods before Me.

"Thou shalt not make unto thee any graven image, or any likeness of anything that is in heaven above, or that is in the earth beneath, or that is in the water under the earth: thou shalt not bow down thyself to them, nor serve them: for I the Lord thy God am a jealous God, visiting the iniquity of the fathers upon the children unto the third and fourth generation of them that hate Me; and shewing mercy unto thousands of them that love Me and keep My commandments.

"Thou shalt not take the name of the Lord thy God in vain; for the Lord will not hold him guiltless that taketh His name in vain.

"Remember the Sabbath day, to keep it holy. Six days shalt thou labour, and do all thy work: but the seventh day is the Sabbath of the Lord thy God: in it thou shalt not do any work, thou, nor thy son, nor thy daughter, thy man-servant, nor thy maid-servant, nor thy cattle, nor thy stranger that is within thy gates: for in six days the Lord made heaven and earth, the sea, and all that in them is, and rested the seventh day: wherefore the Lord blessed the Sabbath day, and hallowed it.

"Honour thy father and thy mother: that thy days may be long upon the land which the Lord thy God giveth thee.

"Thou shalt not kill.

"Thou shalt not commit adultery.

"Thou shalt not steal.

"Thou shalt not bear false witness against thy neighbour.

"Thou shalt not covet thy neighbour's house, thou shalt not covet thy neighbour's wife, nor his man-servant, nor his maid-servant, nor his ox, nor his ass, nor anything that is thy neighbour's" (Exod. xx. 1-17).

2. The Summary of the Law :—

"And one of the scribes asked Him, Which is the first commandment of all? And Jesus answered him, The first commandment is, Hear, O Israel; the Lord our God is one Lord: and thou shalt love the Lord thy God with all thy heart, and with all thy soul, and with all thy mind, and with all thy strength: this is the first commandment. And the second is like, namely this, Thou shalt love thy neighbour as thyself. There is none other commandment greater than these" (Mark xii. 28-31).

3. The Beatitudes :—

"And seeing the multitudes, He went up into a mountain: and when He was set, His disciples came unto Him: and He opened His mouth, and taught them, saying, Blessed are the poor in spirit: for theirs is the kingdom of heaven. Blessed are they that mourn: for they shall be comforted. Blessed are the meek: for they shall inherit the earth. Blessed are they which do hunger and thirst after righteousness : for they shall be filled. Blessed are the merciful: for they shall obtain mercy. Blessed are the pure in heart : for they shall see God. Blessed are the peacemakers : for they shall be called the children of God. Blessed are they which are persecuted for righteousness' sake : for theirs is the kingdom of heaven. Blessed are ye when men shall revile you, and persecute you, and shall say all manner of evil against you falsely, for my sake. Rejoice, and be exceeding glad : for great is your reward in heaven : for so persecuted they the prophets which were before you.

"Ye are the salt of the earth : but if the salt have lost his savour, wherewith shall it be salted ? it is thenceforth good for nothing, but to be cast out, and to be trodden under foot of men. Ye are the light of the world. A city that is set on an hill cannot be hid. Neither do men light a candle, and put it under a bushel, but on a candlestick ; and it giveth light unto all that are in the house. Let your light so shine before men, that they may see your good works, and glorify your Father which is in heaven" (Matt. v. 1-16).

4. The works of the flesh, and the fruit of the Spirit :—

"Now the works of the flesh are manifest, which are these: Adultery, fornication, uncleanness, lasciviousness, idolatry, witchcraft, hatred, variance, emulations, wrath, strife, seditions, heresies, envyings, murders, drunkenness, revellings, and such like : of the which I tell you before, as I have also told you in time past, that they which do such things shall not inherit the kingdom of God. But the fruit of the Spirit is love, joy, peace, long-suffering, gentleness, goodness, faith, meekness, temperance: against such there is no law" (Gal. v. 19-23).

5. Words of Comfort, "For God so loved the world, that He gave His only begotten Son, that whosoever believeth in Him should not perish, but have everlasting life" (John iii. 16); "Come unto me, all ye that labour and are heavy laden, and I will give you rest. Take my yoke upon you, and learn of me; for I am meek and lowly in heart: and ye shall find rest unto your souls. For my yoke is easy, and my burden is light" (Matt. xi. 28-30); "This is a faithful saying, and worthy of all acceptation, that Christ Jesus came into the world to save sinners; of whom I am chief" (1 Tim. i. 15); "There is therefore now no condemnation to them which are in Christ Jesus, who walk not after the flesh, but after the Spirit" (Rom. viii. 1); "My little children, these things write I unto you, that ye sin not. And if any man sin, we have an advocate with the Father, Jesus Christ the righteous: and He is the propitiation for our sins, and not for ours only, but also for the whole world" (1 John ii. 1-2); "Behold, I stand at the door, and knock: if any man hear My voice, and open the door, I will come into him, and will sup with him, and He with me. To him that overcometh will I grant to sit with Me in My throne, even as I also overcame, and am set down with My Father in His throne. He that hath an ear, let him hear what the Spirit saith unto the Churches" (Rev. iii. 20-22).

IV.—Thanksgiving and Consecration Prayer at the Communion.

(*Founded on Westminster Directory, which again draws from Book of Common Order.*)

Heavenly Father, Almighty and Everlasting God, we bless Thee for all Thy mercies to us sinners. We are not worthy of the least of Thy gifts, how much less of the greatest, in that Thou didst give Thine only begotten Son that whosoever believeth in Him should not perish but have everlasting life. We praise Thee for redemption through His blood, the forgiveness of sins, and the eternal inheritance, for the love of God the Father, the Son, and the Spirit, through which redemption comes to us.

Especially we bless Thee this day for the obedience and sacrifice of our Lord Jesus Christ, for all that He purchased for His people, and lives to bestow, for His Word and Sacraments, and for all the ordinances of His house. We give thanks unto Thee for the fellowship of Thy people on earth, and for the memory of Thy saints in heaven. For all Thy servants known to us, who have departed this life in Thy faith and fear, we praise Thee, O God—we beseech Thee that we may be enabled to follow them as they followed Christ. Glory be to Him who is the Resurrection and the Life. Glory be to Him in the Church which waiteth for Him, and in the Church which is around Him.

Heavenly Father, from whom cometh down every good and perfect gift, we bless Thee now for our access to the throne of grace through Jesus Christ, that we are called this day to eat and drink with Him at His Table here, and that we are called to the marriage supper of the Lamb above. We pray Thee, the Father of mercies,

SEC. II.   *THE LORD'S SUPPER.*   141

and the God of all comfort, to grant us now Thy gracious presence, and the effectual working of Thy Holy Spirit in our hearts. Sanctify these elements of bread and wine. And so bless this Thine ordinance to us, that we may receive by faith the body and blood of Christ, even our Lord Jesus Christ Himself, as once crucified for our sins, but now risen and living for our life. May we so feed upon Him this day that He may be one with us, and we one with Him, that He may live in us and we live in Him.

Most gracious God and Father, accept, we beseech Thee, this our sacrifice of praise and thanksgiving, and receive the offering and consecration which we now make of ourselves, our souls and bodies, unto Thee, through Jesus Christ.

And unto Him who loveth us, and hath loosed us from our sins in His own blood, and hath made us kings and priests unto God and His Father, unto Him be the glory and the dominion, for ever and ever. Amen.[1]

V.—PRAYER OF THANKSGIVING AND CONSECRATION.

(*Suggested by, and in part taken from* " *An Order for the Communion,*" *used in St Giles', Edinburgh,* 2nd ed., pp. 163-169.)

Thanksgiving.

Blessed be Thou, O Lord our God, for ever and ever. Thou hast made heaven and earth, the seas, and all

[1] Instead of this closing doxology, the ancient Hymn known as the Ter-Sanctus may be used : And now with Angels and Archangels, and with all the company of heaven, we laud and magnify Thy glorious Name : evermore praising Thee, and saying : Holy, holy, holy, Lord God of hosts, heaven and earth are full of Thy glory : Glory be to Thee, O Lord most High.   Amen.

things that are therein: and Thou preservest them all: and all the host of heaven worshippeth Thee. Thine, O Lord, is the greatness, and the power, and the glory, and the victory, and the majesty: for all that is in the heaven and in the earth is Thine. Now, therefore, our God, we thank Thee, and praise Thy glorious name.

Almighty God, our heavenly Father, we praise and bless Thee for all Thy gifts and benefits towards us; but above all else we thank Thee for Jesus Christ, Thine unspeakable gift. Not as we ought, but as we are able, we praise Thee for His birth in our nature, for His life on earth, for His sufferings and obedience unto death, even the death of the Cross, for His resurrection from the dead, and His ascension to Thy right hand. We give thanks for the coming of the Holy Ghost, and for His abiding Presence and work in the Church and in the world. We praise Thee for the Word and Sacraments, for the fellowship of Thy House on earth, and for the hope of heaven. Blessing and honour and glory and power be unto Him that sitteth upon the Throne, and unto the Lamb, for ever and ever. With Angels and Archangels, and with all the company of heaven, we laud and magnify Thy glorious Name: evermore praising Thee and saying: Holy, holy, holy, Lord God of hosts, heaven and earth are full of Thy glory: Glory be to Thee, O Lord most High.

Prayer of Consecration.

Father of mercies and God of all grace, we beseech Thee draw nigh to each of us now in Thy love, and grant us the effectual working of Thy Holy Spirit in our hearts. Sanctify these elements of bread and wine. And so bless this Thine ordinance that we may receive by faith the body and blood of Jesus Christ crucified for us, with all His benefits, to our spiritual nourishment and growth in grace. Amen.

VI.—Prayer after Communion.

O God, our Heavenly Father, from whom cometh down every good and perfect gift, we give Thee hearty thanks for all the blessings we have received this day at the Lord's Table. Having received Christ Jesus afresh as our Lord and Saviour, may we walk in Him ; may we be rooted and built up in Him, and established in the faith, as we have been taught, abounding therein with thanksgiving. Make Thy grace sufficient for us day by day. Teach us to fight the good fight of faith, to the which we are called, and have professed a good profession before many witnesses. [Here special petitions may be offered for the congregation, the young people, and children present.]

Prayer for the Church Militant.[1]

Remember graciously, O Lord, all those with whom we are one this day in the body of Christ, the multitudes of every name, who are joined with us in the one household of faith, and love, and hope, our brethren and sisters in Christ throughout the world. [Special intercessions may follow for our own Church, and the cause of God in our own land.]

Thanksgiving for the Church Triumphant.[1]

And rejoicing this day in the communion of saints, we bless Thy Holy Name for all Thy servants who, having

---

[1] Taken, with a few slight changes, from " Order of Communion " in St Giles', mentioned above.

accomplished their warfare, are at rest with Thee. We bless Thee for all Thy saints in every age, for those dear to our own souls—our fathers, mothers, brethren and sisters, our dear kindred and friends who have fallen asleep in the Lord. We rejoice to believe that we are still one with them in the same holy fellowship. We pray Thee to enable us so to follow their faith and good example, that we with them may finally be partakers of Thy Heavenly Kingdom at the Coming of our Lord Jesus Christ with all His saints. Hear us, O Heavenly Father, for His sake, to whom, with Thee, and with the Holy Ghost, be glory for ever and ever. Amen.

VII.—ANOTHER PRAYER AFTER COMMUNION.

(*From M. Bersier's " Projet de Révision de la Liturgie des Eglises Réformées de France. Service de Communion—Prière finale.*)

Heavenly Father, Thou hast given us, in the Sacrament of the Lord's Supper, the sign and seal of our being in covenant with Thee through Jesus Christ. Thou hast taken us to be Thy children and Thine inheritance. What shall we render unto Thee for all Thy benefits? Thou hast redeemed us with a great price. May we, therefore, glorify Thee with our bodies and spirits, which are Thine. Be pleased, O Lord, to strengthen us to keep the vows which we have made this day, and to be faithful even unto death. Teach us to do Thy will. May the life that we now live in the flesh be by faith in the Son of God, who loved us and gave Himself for us. May Thy Holy Spirit make us new creatures in Him. Do thou, the God of peace, sanctify us wholly, and may our whole spirit, and soul, and body, be preserved blameless unto the Coming of our Lord Jesus Christ. And unto Him who is able to keep us from falling, and to present us faultless before the presence of His glory with exceeding joy, to the only wise God our Saviour, be glory and majesty, dominion and power, both now and ever. Amen.

Part III.

ORDER OF SERVICES ON SPECIAL OCCASIONS.

Section I.

ADMISSION OF BAPTISED PERSONS TO THE FULL COMMUNION OF THE CHURCH; "YOUNG COMMUNICANTS."

I.—Preparation.

It is of great importance that much care be given to the due Preparation of Candidates for Communion.

1. A Class should be formed by the Minister, at which instruction may be given on such subjects as the following:

The Sacrament of Baptism:

> Its meaning and benefits. Why infants are baptized. The place of the Baptised in the Church. The relation of the Sacrament of Baptism to the Sacrament of the Lord's Supper.

Faith and Repentance:

> How they make Baptism a blessing, and unite us to the Lord Jesus Christ. The work of the Holy Spirit in this, and of our Wills. Conversion. The need of Decision.

The Christian Creed:
> As expressed in The Apostles' Creed, The Nicene Creed, or The Catechisms of the Church.

The Christian Character:
> As in the Ten Commandments, our Lord's Teaching, and the Epistles of the New Testament. The Imitation of Christ. Service in the Kingdom of God.

The Inner Life:
> Prayer. Self-discipline. The need of cultivating the Inward Life.

The Sacrament of the Lord's Supper:
> Its institution. Its meaning. Its order. Its privileges. Its responsibilities.

It is desirable that careful instruction be given concerning the order of The Sacrament; the Thanksgiving Prayer, and the significance of the elements and actions. It will be found a relief to troubled souls, and a profitable exercise to all, to expound with care S. Paul's words in 1 Cor. xi. 27, &c.

At the closing meeting of this Class it will be found helpful to suggest to intending Communicants suitable exercises before Communion: at Communion: and after Communion.

2. The names of candidates for Communion should be made known to the Elders of the District in which they reside, and the Kirk-Session being satisfied of their fitness to receive the full privileges of the Church, a service for their Admission should be publicly intimated, and held.

3. It is not desirable that this service should be conducted in private, or in a hurried way at the close of any other service. It is good that it be held in Church, in presence of the Congregation, the Elders being present with the Minister, and the Candidates being seated together in front of the Communion Table. Experience points to the Sabbath evening before the Communion, the second part of the Friday evening Preparation Service, or the Saturday afternoon or evening before the Communion Sabbath, as suitable times.

II.—Order of Admission Service.

1. Shortened Evening Service.
2. The Names of Candidates read to the Congregation.
3. Questions to Candidates.
4. Prayer.
5. Act of Admission.
6. The Lord's Prayer.
7. Hymn of Consecration.
8. Short Address to Catechumens and to the Congregation.
9. Prayer.
10. Hymn and Benediction.

III.—Notes on Above Order.

1. **Short Evening Service.**

    This Service may be conducted in the usual form, up to the singing of the Anthem or Hymn that follows the second Scripture Lesson.

Appropriate Psalms and Hymns are—

Psalm lxvii; xxv. 4-10; ciii. 13-18: "Holy, Holy, Holy"; "Jesus, Thou Joy of loving hearts"; "Jesus calls us"; "Come, Holy Ghost."

Appropriate Lessons are—

Josh. xxiv. 14-27; Psalm xv.; xvi.; cvii. 1-15; cxvi.; cxix. 1-16; Matt. v. 1-16; John i. 35-46; xxi. 15-22; Rom. xii.; Col. iii. 1-17.

2. **Names of Candidates read,** after which the Minister shall address the Congregation thus:

> These persons have been already received into the visible Church by Baptism; and the Kirk-Session are satisfied as to their knowledge of Christian truth, and as to the sincerity of their profession of faith in Christ. We are now met, therefore, to receive and welcome them to the privileges of full Communion.

3. **Questions to Candidates.**

Next, the Minister shall address the Candidates in these or other suitable words:

> You have been received into the visible Church of Christ by Baptism. You have been instructed in the Faith once delivered to the Saints; and you now desire to take upon you the responsibilities of full membership in the Church, to come to the Table of the Lord, and to partake of all the benefits

which He has appointed for those who are in the membership of "His Body, the Church."

If this is your desire, be pleased to signify it now by standing up.

[All the Candidates stand up.]

A.

The Minister shall then say:

This act implies that you profess your faith in the Lord Jesus Christ, and your desire and purpose henceforth to be His disciple.

"Whosoever shall confess Me before men, him will I confess before My Father in heaven." "With the heart man believeth unto righteousness, and with the mouth confession is made unto salvation."

or, B.

The Minister may say:

Do you believe in God, the Father Almighty, Maker of Heaven and Earth?

And in Jesus Christ, His only Son, our Lord, Who was conceived by the Holy Ghost, born of the Virgin Mary, suffered under Pontius Pilate, was crucified, dead and buried. He descended into Hell (Hades): the third day He rose again from the dead: He ascended into Heaven: and sitteth at the right hand of God the Father Almighty: from thence He shall come to judge the quick and the dead?

Do you believe in the Holy Ghost:

the Holy Catholic Church: the Communion of Saints: the Forgiveness of Sins: the Resurrection of the body: and the Life Everlasting?

Each shall reverently answer, " I do."

[Or the response may be made after each of the three divisions of the Creed.]

The Minister shall continue—

Do you desire to be Christ's disciple; and, in humble dependence on the Holy Spirit, do you promise to trust Him, to follow Him, to learn of Him, and to serve Him unto the end?

Each shall reverently answer, " I do."

4. **Prayer.** Then shall be offered a short Prayer of Thanksgiving for Grace, with special entreaty for the Holy Spirit.

5. **Act of Admission.**

The Minister shall then come near to the Candidates, giving to each "the right hand of fellowship," in name of the Session and Congregation, with words such as these:

M. or N. (naming the person)—

I give thee the right hand of fellowship, receiving thee into the full communion of the visible Church of Christ.

The Lord be with thee.

If it is thought desirable, a text of Scripture may be added.

6. **The Lord's Prayer** may then be said by all.

7. **A Psalm or Hymn of Consecration** shall then be sung, such as—

Psalm cxvi. 1-8, 13-19; cxix. 57-60; "O, Jesus, I have promised"; "I'm not ashamed to own my Lord"; "Jesus, still lead on"; "Rock of Ages"; "O, happy day."

8. **Address.**

The Minister shall then shortly address those who have been received into full Communion, on such subjects as the following :—

Their relation to Christ as the Head of the Church.
Their relation to the Church Catholic.
Their relation to their own Church.
Their relation to their Congregation.
Special features of the Christian Life.
Special graces of the Christian Character.

It will be well to refer to the grace of Liberality : to Temptation : and to the call to Service.

And finally, the Minister shall shortly address the Congregation, bidding them "receive" these new members as Christ has received them "to the glory of God," and calling them to "sanctify" their congregational life, and their personal life, for the brethren's sake.

9. Then shall follow **Prayers for Grace,** and

10. The Service shall conclude in the usual form.

Appropriate Psalms and Hymns are—

Psalm xc. 14-17 ; cxxi.; cxxii. 6-9; "O God

of Bethel"; "Father of peace and God of love."

The plan of this Service should be explained beforehand to the Catechumens.

It will be well if the Minister arrange to meet from time to time in conference those who were prepared by him for Communion, after they have become Communicants, addressing them on some devotional or practical subject, and tenderly enquiring how it fares with them in their Christian life and experience.

Section II.

MARRIAGE.

Whether held in the Church or in the house, it is of great importance that the marriage service be conducted with due solemnity and decorum. It is desirable to return to the ancient custom of the Scottish Church by celebrating marriage, as a rule, "in the place appointed by authority for public worship" (Directory for Public Worship).

It is enacted by Statute that before proceeding to the celebration of marriage the officiating Minister must have evidence produced to him in a Registrar's or Session-Clerk's certificate that notice of marriage has been duly given in the Registrar's Office or the Parish Church.

Order of Service.[1]

       1. Scripture Sentences.
       2. Hymn.
I.   3. Declaration by Minister.
II.   4. Prayer.
III. 5. Vows.
IV. 6. The Marriage Ring.
V.   7. Declaration of Marriage.
VI. 8. Blessing.
VII. 9. Passages from Scripture. ⎱ *or* 9 and 10 may
VIII. 10. Address to Bridegroom ⎰ be taken
          and Bride.   between 4 and 5.
IX. 11. Prayer.
     12. Hymn.
     13. Lord's Prayer.
X. 14. Benediction.

Notes on the Service.

1. Scripture Sentences.

Our help is in the name of the Lord, who made heaven and earth.

Except the Lord build the house, they labour in vain that build it.

Let thy mercy, O Lord, be upon us, according as we hope in Thee.

2. Hymn.

Such Psalms and Hymns are suitable as :—

Ps. c. ; ciii. 1-5 ; cvi. 1-5 ; cxv. 12-18 ; cxxi.

"O God of Bethel," "The Voice that breathed o'er Eden," "O Father, all creating."

---

[1] The shorter form, indicated by the figures on the left, may suffice for marriages in the house.

The Bride, with Bridal party, enters the Church and takes her place on the left hand of the Bridegroom before the commencement of the Service, while a wedding march is played; or she and they may enter during the singing of the first hymn. In that case 1 and 2 are transposed, the hymn coming first, and the Scripture sentence being spoken by the Minister before he begins his declaration.

3. Declaration by Minister.

The Minister may use these or like words:—We are here met in the sight of God and in the face of this congregation [before these witnesses] to join together this man and this woman in the honourable estate of matrimony.

Marriage is a divine ordinance whose sanctity is to be jealously guarded. It is the foundation of the Christian home with its priceless blessings. It is ordained for the mutual help and comfort of husband and wife, and their edification in the Christian life. The sacredness of the marriage bond is used in Scripture as a fitting symbol of the mystical union between Christ and His Church.

Into this holy estate these two persons now desire to enter, and no reason has been alleged why they may not lawfully be joined together. Let us therefore unite in prayer for God's blessing on what is now to be done in His Name.

4. Prayer.

All kneeling; the Bridegroom and Bride, with their immediate friends, in front of the Communion Table, if that can be conveniently arranged.

The prayer may include—

(1) Thanksgiving for God's manifold goodness; His

love towards sinners in Jesus Christ; the gladness of human life; the sympathies which bind us to each other; the joys of family affection; the sacred influences of the Christian home; the love of husband and wife; the strength and comfort of Christian marriage.

(2) Supplication for the Bride and Bridegroom, that they may have the aid of God's Spirit to make their vows to each other in His strength and fear; and that God, "whose presence is the happiness of every condition, and sweetens every relation, would be their portion; and that as He hath brought them together by His providence, He would sanctify them by His Spirit, giving them a new frame of heart fit for their new estate, enriching them with all graces, whereby they may perform the duties, enjoy the comforts, undergo the cares, and resist the temptations which accompany that condition as becometh Christians."

5. Vows.

All standing. The congregation should be reminded of this, if needful.

The Minister shall say to the Bridegroom and Bride:—

In token of the covenant which you are now about to make, take each other by the right hand.

The Minister shall say to the Bridegroom:—

Do you, A. B., take C. D., to be your wedded wife, and do you, in the presence of God and before this congregation [these witnesses], promise and covenant to be to her a loving, faithful and dutiful husband, until God shall separate you by death?

The Bridegroom shall answer—

I do.

The Minister shall say to the Bride :—

Do you, C. D., take A. B., whom you hold by the hand, to be your wedded husband; and do you, in the presence of God and before this congregation, promise and covenant to be to him a loving, faithful and dutiful wife, until God shall separate you by death?

The Bride shall answer—

I do.

[*In the Directory the vows made by Bridegroom and Bride do not take the form of a response to questions by the Minister, but are a direct statement in the first person, the words being repeated after the Minister.*]

6. The Marriage Ring.

The Bridegroom and Bride shall loose hands, and the Minister shall say :—

As a pledge of the covenant you have made with each other, the marriage ring is now given and received.

The Bridegroom shall place the ring on the third finger of the Bride's left hand.

7. Declaration of Marriage.

The Minister shall say :—

I declare these two to be husband and wife, In the name of the Father, of the Son, and of the Holy Ghost.

Whom therefore God hath joined together, let not man put asunder.

8. Blessing.

The Minister may say :—

The grace of the Lord Jesus Christ, the love of God, and the communion of the Holy Ghost be with you.

or,

The Lord sanctify and bless you; the Lord pour the

riches of His grace upon you, that you may please Him, and live together in holy love to your lives' end.

The Anthem " The Lord bless you," *may then be sung. All standing.*

9. Passages from Scripture.

The Minister may read passages of Scripture bearing on the duties of husbands and wives.

Ephes. v. 22-33 ; 1 Pet. iii. 1-7.
Col. iii. 12-19.
1 Cor. xiii. 4-7 ; Matt. xix. 4-6.

10. Address.

The Minister may add a brief address on such topics as these: the consecration of wedded life by love to God, marriage as a means of grace, the sanctification of the life of the home, mutual encouragement in the service of Christ, the cultivation of conjugal love by sympathy, trustfulness, patience, forbearance, mutual consideration, and thoughtfulness.

11. Prayer.

This prayer may include—

(1) Thanksgiving on behalf of the Bridegroom and Bride for the enrichment and enlargement of life which God in His goodness has bestowed upon them.

(2) Supplication that they may be faithful to their new responsibilities, that their love for each other rooted in the love of Christ may grow in strength, that as heirs together of the grace of life they may encourage each other in all godly living and Christian service, that Christ's presence may sanctify their new home, and be their strength and comfort amid temptations and trials, that they may fulfil God's holy will in this life, and be prepared for His service and His joy in the life to come.

12. **Praise.**
Psalms cxxi.; lxvii.; cxxv. 1 and 2; cxxxvi. (2nd Version), 1-4, 23-26.
Hymns: "How welcome was the call," "O perfect love," "O happy home," "Now thank we all our God."

13. **The Lord's Prayer.**
At the close of the service the Lord's Prayer may suitably be used.

14. **Benediction.**
Thereafter the Bridal party pass into the Vestry for the necessary signatures, the congregation being asked to keep their seats till their return. On their re-appearance, the wedding march is begun. All now rise, and remain standing until the Bridal company have passed out of the Church.

APPENDIX.

Marriage Service.

(*from Hermann's "Consultation," ed.* 1545. *Slightly shortened and adapted.*)

The Minister shall say to the Bridegroom and Bride:—
You are here present before God our Father and our Lord Jesus Christ, and in the face of this congregation of His people, to plight your faith publicly one to another in marriage, and to seek the blessing of the Lord thereon, through the Ministry of His Church. Is not this your purpose and desire?

Answer: It is.

Then the Minister shall say further:—
Seeing then that, after open publication of this your urpose, no one hath come forward to gainsay the same,

or to allege any lawful impediment to your being joined together in holy wedlock, may our heavenly Father be pleased to confirm and bless that which we now do in His name. And that ye may the better understand what marriage in the Lord is, hear first how it was ordained of God in the beginning:

"And the Lord God took the man, and put him into the garden of Eden to dress it and to keep it. . . . And the Lord God said: It is not good that the man should be alone; I will make him an help meet for him. . . . And the Lord God caused a deep sleep to fall upon Adam, and he slept; and He took one of his ribs and closed up the flesh instead thereof; and the rib, which the Lord God had taken from man, made He a woman, and brought her unto the man. And Adam said: This is now bone of my bones and flesh of my flesh: she shall be called woman, because she was taken out of man. Therefore shall a man leave his father and his mother and shall cleave unto his wife; and they shall be one flesh." [1]

Now hear ye the voice of Christ out of the Gospel:

"The Pharisees came unto Him, tempting Him, and saying unto Him: Is it lawful for a man to put away his wife for every cause? And He answered and said unto them: Have ye not read that He which made them at the beginning made them male and female, and said: For this cause shall a man leave father and mother and cleave to his wife; and they twain shall be one flesh? Wherefore they are no more twain, but one flesh. What therefore God hath joined together, let not man put asunder." [2]

Hear also the commandment of the Holy Ghost by the Apostle Paul concerning the duties of marriage, for thus he prescribeth to married folk:

[1] Gen. ii. 15, 18-24. [2] Matt. xix. 3-6.

"Wives, submit yourselves unto your own husbands as unto the Lord. For the husband is the head of the wife, even as Christ is the head of the Church; and He is the Saviour of the body. Therefore as the Church is subject unto Christ, so let the wives be to their own husbands in every thing. Husbands, love your wives, even as Christ also loved the Church and gave Himself for it. So ought men to love their wives as their own bodies. He that loveth his wife loveth himself. For no man ever yet hated his own flesh; but nourisheth and cherisheth it, even as the Lord the Church: for we are members of His body, of His flesh and of His bones. For this cause shall a man leave his father and mother and shall be joined unto his wife, and they two shall be one flesh. This is a great mystery: but I speak concerning Christ and the Church. Nevertheless, let every one of you in particular so love his wife even as himself; and the wife see that she reverence her husband."[1]

Consider then, dearly beloved, how holy a kind of life, and how acceptable to God matrimony is. For by these Scriptures we know that God Himself instituted holy wedlock, and that in Paradise, man being yet upright and without sin. Also He hath greatly blessed this estate, and Himself joineth together all those who are wedded in His name. For he giveth the husband to be an head and helper to the wife, even as Christ is the Head and Saviour of the Church; and giveth also the wife to be an help meet, yea, even another self, unto the husband, so that here in this world they may lead a godly, honest, and joyous life together.

God is Love; and he that dwelleth in love dwelleth in God. Also the whole law is fulfilled in this, that we

[1] Ephes. v. 22-33.

love our neighbour as ourselves. But there is no surer faithfulness, no warmer love, no nearer friendship, no prompter will to serve one another than that which is among such married folk as be joined together in the Lord, and among their children, and all those whom marriage hath thus allied together on both sides. Wherefore all they whom God hath thus united ought to give great thanks unto Him for this so great a benefit, that He hath called them to so holy and blessed a kind of life, and so acceptable to Himself.

Neither must the husband otherwise receive his wife, nor the wife her husband, than as given, each to each, by the Lord's own hand. And whatsoever trouble or adversity may befall them in married life, let them flee to God with sure confidence, and seek help and comfort from Him. For our most loving Father will not forsake His children in that kind of life in which He Himself hath set them. He cannot but assuage the difficulties, and uphold under the exercises of obedience, which He seeth good to appoint for them in this estate, to try and to stir up their faith, and not to afflict them.

Let exhortation be given after this fashion, in more or fewer words, according as the case seemeth to require. Thereafter, let prayer be made, that God would bless these twain now to be joined together in marriage, and would grant unto them both to begin aright now, and to hold fast to their life's end all the commands and counsels given them from the Word of God. *Then, after a brief space allowed for silent prayer in the Church, the Minister shall cause the Bridegroom and the Bride to join hands, and shall say to the Bridegroom :—*

John N., hast thou then determined, before the Lord, to take Anne N. to be thy wife in the Lord, and so to live with her all thy days, as thou heardest even now that it is required of a Christian husband?

Answer—I have so determined, trusting in the Lord's help.

Then shall he say to the Bride:—

Anne N., hast thou also determined, before the Lord, to take John N. to be thy husband in the Lord, and so to live with him all thy days, as thou heardest even now that it is required of a Christian wife?

Answer—I have so determined, trusting in the Lord's help.

Then shall the wedding ring be put by the Bridegroom on the third finger of the Bride's left hand, and the Minister, making them to join their right hands, shall say:—Whom God hath joined together, let not man put asunder; *and shall add with a loud voice so that all may hear:* Forasmuch as these twain have plighted their troth to each other as husband and wife before God and this congregation, as ye have heard and seen them do, I, therefore, as a Minister of Christ and of His Church, hereby declare that they are joined together in lawful and Christian marriage in the name of the Father, the Son, and the Holy Ghost. Amen.

Then let a Psalm or Hymn be sung, and thereafter let the Minister conclude the whole matter with prayer.

Section III.

THE BURIAL OF THE DEAD.

The following selection of Scripture passages is arranged under four heads—Mortality, Confidence in God, The Resurrection, Victory; and it will perhaps be found convenient in most cases to read from each of the four. In this way, an ascent will be made from sorrow over the dead to triumph over death in Jesus Christ.

Although the Service will usually be in private, there will come occasions when it must be public, and when, in addition to reading and prayer, the congregation may engage in singing. The following order may then be observed :—

Prayer.
Singing.
Reading from Old Testament (i., ii.).
Prayer.
Singing.
Reading from New Testament (iii., iv.).
Prayer.
Singing.
Benediction.

Such Psalms and Hymns as these may be sung—

Psalms: xc. 1-4, 14-17; xci. 14-16; cii. 2nd Version, 23-8; ciii. 13-18; cxxi.; xxxix. 4-12; lxii. 5-8; xxiii.

Hymns: "A few more years shall roll"; "For ever with the Lord"; "The sands of time"; "Now the labourer's task is o'er"; "Brief life is here our portion"; "Now lay we calmly in the grave"; "Gentle Shepherd, Thou hast stilled"; "Safely, safely gathered in"; "For all the saints"; "Come let us join our friends above"; "How bright these glorious spirits shine."

With regard to the prayers offered at this Service either in public or private, the main point to be observed is, that while they naturally start from the frailty of man and the sorrow of such a moment, they should chiefly dwell upon the grace and power of Christ who has brought life and immortality to light by the Gospel. It is this which ought to occupy the mind of believers in the presence of death, as it is this that affords them comfort. And it is the comfort of the mourning, not pathos, that is the end and aim of the Service.

It may seem necessary sometimes to make more distinct reference to the life or the work of the deceased, but such reference ought to be made with the utmost reserve and delicacy. For the laudation of any one, however saintly, in words addressed to Him who knows the heart, can hardly be appropriate.

The service at the grave, when there is one, ought, above all things, especially in view of our climate, to be short, and confined to a sentence or two from Scripture and a few words of prayer, which, if well chosen, will be none the less impressive that they are few.

I.—Mortality.

Job xiv. 1, 2, 11, 12.
Man that is born of a woman is of few days, and full of trouble. He cometh forth like a flower and is cut down: he fleeth also as a shadow and continueth not. Man dieth and wasteth away: yea, man giveth up the ghost, and where is he? As the waters fail from the sea, and the river decayeth and drieth up, so man lieth down and riseth not: Till the heavens be no more, they shall not awake, nor be roused out of their sleep.

Job iii. 17, 18, 19.
There the wicked cease from troubling, and there the weary be at rest. There the prisoners are at ease together: they hear not the voice of the taskmaster.

The small and great are there: and the servant is free from his master.

As the cloud is consumed and vanisheth away, so Job vii. 9, 10.
he that goeth down to the grave shall come up no more.
He shall return no more to his house, neither shall his
place know him any more.

It is appointed unto men once to die, but after this Heb. ix. 27.
the judgment.

By one man sin entered into the world, and death by Rom. v. 12.
sin; and so death passed upon all men, for that all
have sinned.

Lord, make me to know mine end, and the measure Ps. xxxix. 4-6.
of my days, what it is; let me know how frail I am.
Behold thou hast made my days as an handbreadth, and
mine age is as nothing before thee: surely every man at
his best state is altogether vanity. Surely every man
walketh in a vain show: surely they are disquieted in
vain. When thou with rebukes dost correct man for
iniquity, thou makest his beauty to consume away like a
moth. Surely every man is vanity.

Lord, thou hast been our dwelling-place in all genera- Ps. xc. 1-8.
tions. Before the mountains were brought forth, or
ever thou hadst formed the earth and the world, even
from everlasting to everlasting thou art God. Thou
turnest man to destruction, and sayest, Return, ye
children of men. For a thousand years in thy sight
are but as yesterday when it is past, and as a watch in
the night. Thou carriest them away as with a flood;
they are as a sleep: In the morning they are like grass
which groweth up: in the morning it flourisheth and

Ps. xc. 9, 10.
groweth up: in the evening it is cut down and withereth. We spend our years as a tale that is told. The days of our years are threescore years and ten; and if by reason of strength they be fourscore years, yet is their strength labour and sorrow: for it is soon cut off and we fly away. So teach us to number our days, that we may apply our hearts unto wisdom. O satisfy us early with thy mercy that we may rejoice and be glad all our days.

12.
14.

Ps. ciii. 13-17.
Like as a father pitieth his children, so the Lord pitieth them that fear him. For he knoweth our frame: he remembereth that we are dust. As for man, his ways are as grass: as a flower of the field so he flourisheth. For the wind passeth over it and it is gone, and the place thereof shall know it no more. But the mercy of the Lord is from everlasting to everlasting upon them that fear him, and his righteousness unto children's children.

Eccles. xii. 1-7.
Remember now thy Creator in the days of thy youth, while the evil days come not, nor the years draw nigh, when thou shalt say, I have no pleasure in them; while the sun, and the light, and the moon, and the stars be not darkened; nor the clouds return after the rain: in the day when the keepers of the house shall tremble, and the strong men shall bow themselves, and the grinders cease because they are few, and those that look out of the windows be darkened, and the doors shall be shut in the street, when the sound of the grinding is low, and one shall rise up at the voice of a bird, and all the daughters of music shall be brought low. Yea, they shall be afraid of that which is high, and fears shall be in the way: and the almond tree shall flourish, and the grasshopper

shall be a burden, and desire shall fail, because man goeth to his long home, and the mourners go about the streets: or ever the silver cord be loosed, or the golden bowl be broken, or the pitcher be broken at the fountain, or the wheel broken at the cistern. Then shall the dust return to the earth as it was, and the spirit shall return unto God who gave it.

It came to pass the seventh day that the child died; and the servants of David feared to tell him that the child was dead. But when David saw that the servants whispered, he perceived that the child was dead (therefore David said unto the servants, is the child dead? and they said, He is dead.) Then David arose from the earth, and washed and anointed himself, and changed his apparel, and came into the house of the Lord and worshipped: then he came to his own house; and he did eat. Then said his servants unto him, What is this that thou hast done? thou didst fast and weep for the child while it was alive; but when the child was dead thou dost arise and eat bread. And he said, while the child was yet alive I fasted and wept; for I said, who can tell whether God will be gracious to me that the child may live? But now he is dead, wherefore should I fast? can I bring him back again? I shall go to him, but he shall not return to me. *2 Sam. xii. 18-23.*

Suffer the little children to come to me, and forbid them not. I say unto you that in heaven their angels do always behold the face of my Father who is in Heaven. *Mark x. 14. Matt. xviii. 10.*

He shall feed His flock like a shepherd, He shall gather the lambs in His arms and carry them in His bosom. *Isaiah xl. 11.*

Luke vii. 11-16. And it came to pass that He went into a city called Nain, and many of His disciples went with Him, and much people. Now when He came nigh to the gate of the city, behold, there was a dead man carried out, the only son of his mother, and she was a widow: and much people of the city was with her. And when the Lord saw her, He had compassion on her, and said unto her, Weep not. And He came and touched the bier: and they that bare him stood still, and He said, Young man, I say unto thee, arise. And he that was dead sat up and began to speak. And He delivered him to his mother. And there came a fear on all, and they glorified God, saying, That a great prophet is risen up among us, and, That God hath visited His people.

John xi. 32-35. Then when Mary was come where Jesus was, and saw Him, she fell down at His feet, saying unto Him, Lord, if Thou hadst been here, my brother had not died. When Jesus therefore saw her weeping, and the Jews also weeping, which came with her, He groaned in the spirit and was troubled, and said, Where have ye laid him? They said unto Him, Lord, come and see. Jesus wept.

II.—CONFIDENCE IN GOD.

Job ii. 10.
Ps. xxxix. 9.
1 Sam. iii. 18.
Shall we receive good at the hand of God, and shall we not receive evil? I was dumb, I opened not my mouth, because Thou didst it. It is the Lord, let Him do what seemeth Him good.

Ps. xxiii. The Lord is my shepherd: I shall not want. He maketh me to lie down in green pastures; He leadeth

SEC. III.]   *BURIAL OF THE DEAD.*   171

me beside the still waters. He restoreth my soul: He leadeth me in the paths of righteousness for His name's sake. Yea, though I walk through the valley of the shadow of death I will fear no evil; for Thou art with me; Thy rod and Thy staff they comfort me. Thou preparest a table before me in the presence of mine enemies: Thou anointest my head with oil; my cup runneth over. Surely goodness and mercy shall follow me all the days of my life; and I will dwell in the house of the Lord for ever.

The eyes of the Lord are upon the righteous, and His ears are open unto their cry. The Lord is nigh unto them that are of a broken heart; and saveth such as be of a contrite spirit. Many are the afflictions of the righteous: but the Lord delivereth him out of them all. He keepeth all his bones: not one of them is broken. The Lord redeemeth the soul of His servants: and none of them that trust in Him shall be desolate. *Ps. xxxiv. 15, 18, 19, 22.*

God is our refuge and strength, a very present help in trouble. Therefore will not we fear, though the earth be removed, and though the mountains be carried into the midst of the sea; though the waters thereof roar and be troubled; though the mountains shake with the swelling thereof. There is a river, the streams whereof shall make glad the city of God, the holy place of the tabernacle of the most high. God is in the midst of her; she shall not be moved; God shall help her and that right early. *Ps. xlvi. 1-5.*

He that dwelleth in the secret place of the Most *Ps. xci. 1-4.*

High shall abide under the shadow of the Almighty. I will say of the Lord, He is my refuge and my fortress; my God, in Him will I trust. He shall cover thee with His feathers, and under His wings shalt thou trust; His truth shall be thy shield and buckler.

Ps. xci. 9-1*.

Because thou hast made the Lord which is my refuge, even the Most High, thy habitation, there shall no evil befall thee, neither shall any plague come nigh thy dwelling. For He shall give his angels charge over thee, to keep thee in all thy ways. They shall bear thee up in their hands, lest thou dash thy foot against a stone.

4-16.

Because he hath set his love upon me, therefore will I deliver him: I will set him on high, because he hath known my name. He shall call upon Me, and I will answer him: I will be with him in trouble; I will deliver him and honour him. With long life will I satisfy him, and show him My salvation.

Ps. ciii. 1-5.

Bless the Lord, O my soul; and all that is within me, bless His holy name. Bless the Lord, O my soul, and forget not all His benefits, who forgiveth all thine iniquities, who healeth all thy diseases, who redeemeth thy life from destruction, who crowneth thee with loving-kindness and tender mercies, who satisfieth thy mouth with good things, so that thy youth is renewed like the eagle's.

8-13.

The Lord is merciful and gracious, slow to anger, and plenteous in mercy. He will not always chide; neither will He keep His anger for ever. He hath not dealt with us after our sins, nor rewarded us according to our iniquities. For as the heaven is high above the earth, so great is His mercy toward them that fear Him. As far as the east is from the west, so far hath He removed our transgressions from us. Like as a father pitieth his children, so the Lord pitieth them that fear Him.

Hear my prayer, O Lord, give ear to my supplications; in Thy faithfulness answer me, and in Thy righteousness. For my spirit is overwhelmed within me, my heart within me is desolate. I stretch forth my hands unto Thee; my soul thirsteth after Thee, as a thirsty land. Hear me speedily, O Lord, my spirit faileth; hide not Thy face from me, lest I be like unto them that go down to the pit. Cause me to hear Thy lovingkindness in the morning, for in Thee do I trust; cause me to know the way wherein I should walk, for I lift up my soul unto Thee. It is of the Lord's mercies that we are not consumed, because his compassions fail not. They are new every morning, great is Thy faithfulness. The Lord is good unto them that wait upon Him, to the soul that seeketh Him. The Lord will not cast off for ever; but though He cause grief, yet will He have compassion according to the multitude of his mercies. But He doth not afflict willingly, nor grieve the children of men. *Ps. cxliii. 1, 4, 6, 7, 8.* *Lam. iii. 22.* *Ps. xliv. 23.* *Lam. iii. 33.*

Our light affliction, which is but for a moment, worketh for us a far more exceeding and eternal weight of glory; while we look not at the things which are seen, but at the things which are not seen, for the things which are seen are temporal, but the things which are not seen are eternal. *2 Cor. iv. 17, 18.*

Heb. xii. 7, 11.   If ye endure chastening, God dealeth with you as sons. Now, no chastening for the present seemeth to be joyous, but grievous, nevertheless afterward it yieldeth the peaceable fruit of righteousness.

III.—Resurrection and Eternal Life.

Job xix. 25, 26.   I know that my Redeemer liveth, and that He shall stand at the latter day upon the earth; and tho' after my skin worms destroy this body, yet in my flesh shall I see God.

1 Cor. xv. 21-28.   Since by man came death, by man came also the resurrection of the dead. For as in Adam all die, even so in Christ shall all be made alive. But every man in his own order: Christ the first-fruits; afterward they that are Christ's at His coming. Then cometh the end, when He shall have delivered up the Kingdom to God, even the Father; when He shall have put down all rule and all authority and power. For He must reign till He hath put all enemies under His feet. The last enemy that shall be destroyed is death. For He hath put all things under His feet. But when He saith all things are put under Him, it is manifest that He is excepted, which did put all things under Him. And when all things shall be subdued unto Him, then shall the Son also Himself be subject unto Him that put all things under Him, that God may be all in all.

42-44.   It is sown in corruption; it is raised in incorruption; it is sown in dishonour; it is raised in glory; it is sown in weakness; it is raised in power; it is sown a natural body; it is raised a spiritual body. . . . Now this I say,

50-58.

SEC. III.] BURIAL OF THE DEAD. 175

brethren, that flesh and blood cannot inherit the Kingdom of God; neither doth corruption inherit incorruption. Behold, I show you a mystery; we shall not all sleep, but we shall all be changed, in a moment, in the twinkling of an eye, at the last trump; for the trumpet shall sound, and the dead shall be raised incorruptible, and we shall be changed. For this corruptible must put on incorruption, and this mortal must put on immortality. So when this corruption shall have put on incorruption, and this mortal shall have put on immortality, then shall be brought to pass the saying that is written, Death is swallowed up in victory. O death, where is thy sting? O grave, where is thy victory? The sting of death is sin, and the strength of sin is the law. But thanks be to God, which giveth us the victory through our Lord Jesus Christ. Therefore, my beloved brethren, be ye steadfast, unmoveable, always abounding in the work of the Lord, forasmuch as ye know that your labour is not in vain in the Lord.

But I would not have you ignorant, brethren, concerning them which are asleep, that ye sorrow not, even as others which have no hope. For if we believe that Jesus died and rose again, even so them also which sleep in Jesus will God bring with Him. For this we say unto you by the word of the Lord, that we which are alive and remain unto the coming of the Lord shall not prevent them which are asleep. For the Lord Himself shall descend from heaven with a shout, with the voice of the archangel, and with the trump of God: and the dead in Christ shall rise first: then we which are alive and remain shall be caught up together with them in the clouds, to meet the Lord in

1 Thessal. iv. 13-18.

the air: and so shall we ever be with the Lord. Wherefore comfort one another with these words.

1 Pet. i. 3-8.
Blessed be the God and Father of our Lord Jesus Christ, which according to His abundant mercy hath begotten us again unto a living hope by the resurrection of Jesus Christ from the dead, to an inheritance incorruptible and undefiled and that fadeth not away, reserved in heaven for you who are kept by the power of God through faith unto salvation ready to be revealed in the last time. Wherein ye greatly rejoice, though now for a season, if need be, ye are in heaviness through manifold trials; that the trying of your faith, being much more precious than of gold that perisheth, though it be tried with fire, might be found unto praise and honour and glory at the appearing of Jesus Christ: whom having not seen ye love: in whom, though now ye see Him not, yet believing, ye rejoice with joy unspeakable and full of glory.

John xiv. 1-3.

18, 19.

27.
Let not your heart be troubled: ye believe in God, believe also in Me. In My Father's house are many mansions; if it were not so, I would have told you. I go to prepare a place for you. And if I go and prepare a place for you, I will come again and receive you unto Myself: that where I am, there ye may be also. I will not leave you comfortless, I will come to you. Yet a little while, and the world seeth Me no more: but ye see me: Because I live ye shall live also. Peace I leave with you, My peace I give unto you; not as the world giveth, give I unto you. Let not your heart be troubled, neither let it be afraid.

2 Cor. v. 1.
For we know that if our earthly house of this tabernacle were dissolved we have a building of God, an

house not made with hands, eternal in the heavens. Therefore we are always confident, knowing that, whilst we are at home in the body, we are absent from the Lord, for we walk by faith not by sight: we are confident, I say, and willing rather to be absent from the body and to be present with the Lord. Wherefore we labour, that, whether present or absent, we may be accepted of Him. For we must all appear before the judgment seat of Christ, that every one may receive the things done in his body, according to that he hath done, whether it be good or bad. 2 Cor. v. 6-10.

IV.—VICTORY.

Who shall separate us from the love of Christ? Shall tribulation, or distress, or persecution, or famine, or nakedness, or peril, or sword? Nay, in all these things we are more than conquerors through Him that loved us. For I am persuaded that neither death, nor life, nor angels, nor principalities, nor powers, nor things present, nor things to come, nor height, nor depth, nor any other creature, shall be able to separate us from the love of God which is in Christ Jesus our Lord. Rom. viii. 35-39.

After this I beheld, and lo, a great multitude which no man can number, of all nations, and kindreds, and people, and tongues stood before the throne and before the Lamb, clothed with white robes, and palms in their hands: and cried with a loud voice saying, Salvation to our God which sitteth upon the throne, and unto the Lamb. And all the angels stood round about the throne, and about the elders and the four living creatures, and fell before the throne on their faces, and worshipped God, saying, Amen; Blessing, and glory, and wisdom, Rev. vii. 9-17.

and thanksgiving, and honour, and power, and might, be unto our God for ever and ever. Amen. And one of the elders answered, saying unto me, What are these which are arrayed in white robes? and whence came they? And I said unto him, Sir, thou knowest. And he said to me, These are they which came out of great tribulation, and have washed their robes and made them white in the blood of the Lamb. Therefore are they before the throne of God, and serve Him day and night in His temple; and He that sitteth on the throne shall dwell among them. They shall hunger no more, neither thirst any more; neither shall the sun light on them, nor any heat. For the Lamb which is in the midst of the throne shall feed them, and shall lead them unto living fountains of waters; and God shall wipe away all tears from their eyes.

Rev. xx. 11-14. And I saw a great white throne, and him that sat on it, from whose face the earth and the heaven fled away: and there was found no place for them. And I saw the dead, small and great, stand before God; and the books were opened: and another book was opened which was the book of life: and the dead were judged out of those things which were written in the books according to their works. And the sea gave up the dead which were in it; and death and hell delivered up the dead which were in them: and they were judged every man according to their works. And death and hell were cast into the lake of fire.

Rev. xxi. 1-5. And I saw a new heaven and a new earth: for the first heaven and the first earth were passed away; and there was no more sea. And I, John, saw the holy city, new Jerusalem, coming down from God out of heaven, prepared as a bride adorned for her husband.

And I heard a great voice out of heaven, saying, Behold, the tabernacle of God is with men, and he will dwell with them, and they shall be his people, and God himself shall be with them and be their God. And God shall wipe away all tears from their eyes; and there shall be no more death, neither sorrow nor crying, neither shall there be any more pain; for the former things are passed away. And he that sat upon the throne said, Behold, I make all things new.

And he shewed me a river of water of life, clear as Rev. xxii. 1-5. crystal proceeding out of the throne of God and of the Lamb. In the midst of the street of it and on either side of the river was there the tree of life, which bare twelve manner of fruits, and yielded her fruit every month: and the leaves of the tree were for the healing of the nations. And there shall be no more curse: but the throne of God and of the Lamb shall be in it; and his servants shall serve him. And they shall see his face; and his name shall be in their foreheads. And there shall be no night there; and they need no light of lamp, neither light of the sun; for the Lord God giveth them light: and they shall reign for ever and ever.

At the Grave.

What profit hath a man of all the labour which Eccles. i. 3, 4 he taketh under the sun? One generation passeth away 8, 11. and another generation cometh: but the earth abideth for ever. All things are full of weariness; man cannot utter it: the eye is not satisfied with seeing, nor the ear filled with hearing. There is no remembrance of the former generations: neither shall there be any remembrance of the latter generations that are to come among

Eccles. viii. 8. those that shall come after. There is no man that hath power over the spirit to retain the spirit: neither hath he power over the day of death, and there is no discharge in that war.

Pet. i. 24, 25. All flesh is grass, and all the goodliness thereof is as the flower of the field: the grass withereth, the flower fadeth, because the spirit of the Lord bloweth upon it: surely the people is grass. The grass withereth, the flower fadeth: but the word of our God shall stand for ever.

Gen. iii. 19. Dust thou art, and unto dust shalt thou return. But God will redeem my soul from the power of the grave, for He shall receive me.
Ps. xlix. 15.

John v. 28, 29. The hour is coming in the which all that are in the graves shall hear His voice, and shall come forth: they that have done good unto the resurrection of life, and they that have done evil unto the resurrection of judgment.

John vi. 39. This is the Father's will who hath sent me, that of all which He hath given me I should lose nothing, but should raise it up at the last day.

Pet. iii. 8-10. Forget not this one thing, beloved, that one day is with the Lord as a thousand years, and a thousand years as one day. The Lord is not slack concerning His promise, as some count slackness: but is longsuffering to you-ward, not wishing that any should perish, but that all should come to repentance. But the day of the Lord will come as a thief in the night.

Heb. xiii. 20, 21. Now, the God of peace, that brought again from the dead our Lord Jesus Christ, that great Shepherd of the sheep, through the blood of the everlasting covenant, made you perfect in every good work to do His will, working in you that which is well-pleasing in His sight,

BURIAL OF THE DEAD.

through Jesus Christ, to whom be glory for ever and ever. Amen.

As for me, I will behold Thy face in righteousness : I shall be satisfied when I awake with Thy likeness. Ps. xvii. 15.
Thou wilt show me the path of life; in Thy presence is fulness of joy; at Thy right hand there are pleasures for evermore. Ps. xvi. 11.

We know that if our earthly house of this tabernacle were dissolved, we have a building of God, an house not made with hands, eternal in the heavens. 2 Cor. v. 1.

Our Lord Jesus Christ died for us that, whether we wake or sleep, we should live together with Him. 1 Thessal. v. 10.

I heard a voice from heaven saying unto me, Write, Blessed are the dead which die in the Lord from henceforth : yea, saith the Spirit, that they may rest from their labours ; and their works do follow them. Rev. xiv. 13.

Jesus saith, I am the Resurrection and the Life ; he that believeth in Me, though he were dead, yet shall he live : and whosoever liveth and believeth in Me shall never die. John xi. 25.

So teach us to number our days that we may apply our hearts unto wisdom. Ps. xc. 12.

Whether we live, we live unto the Lord ; and whether we die, we die unto the Lord : whether we live therefore, or die, we are the Lord's. Rom. xiv. 8.

Here have we no continuing city, but we seek one to come. Heb. xiii. 14.

Luke xii. 35-38. Let your loins be girded about, and your lights burning; and ye yourselves like unto men that wait for their Lord, when He will return from the wedding; that, when He cometh and knocketh, they may open unto Him immediately. Blessed are those servants whom the Lord, when He cometh, shall find watching: verily I say unto you, that He shall gird Himself, and make them to sit down to meat, and will come forth and serve them. And if He shall come in the second watch, or come in the third watch, and find them so, blessed are those servants.

APPENDIX.

For the service at the grave, two or three suitable sentences may be read, and then prayer offered in such words as the following:—

I.

Almighty and everlasting God, the Father of our Lord Jesus Christ, who in Thy holy providence hast called us together at this time, grant, we pray Thee, that as Thy blessed Son came unto the sisters who mourned for their beloved laid in the grave at Bethany, so by Thy gracious Spirit He may be revealed in the midst of us, saying, "I am the resurrection and the life: he that believeth in Me, though he were dead, yet shall he live: and whosoever liveth and believeth in Me shall never die." And since Jesus Christ is the same yesterday and to-day and for ever, may we, in this our day of sorrow, receive of Thee everlasting consolation and good hope through grace in the name of Him who is gone to that house of Thine where are many mansions, there to prepare a place for us.

Unto Thee, Father of lights, from whom cometh every good and every perfect gift, we render unto Thee our heartfelt thanks for the work of faith and labour of love, and patience of hope of our brother (sister) departed. We give thanks unto Thee, who forgivest all our iniquities and healest all our diseases, forasmuch as Thou hast in Thy great mercy granted unto him (her) release from the pain of this life, its weakness, and its sorrow. Now returneth the dust to the earth as it was, and the spirit is returned unto God who gave it. We bless Thy holy name, for if we believe that Jesus died and rose again, even so them also which sleep in Jesus Thou wilt bring with Him.

O God, who hast not appointed us unto wrath, but to obtain salvation through our Lord Jesus Christ, grant unto us that as He died for us, so whether we wake or sleep, we may live together with Him. The night is far spent, the day is at hand. Enable us therefore to cast off the works of darkness and to put on the armour of light. As Thou hast brought life and immortality to light through the gospel, destroying the face of the covering cast over all people, and the veil that was spread over all nations, teach us to be steadfast, immoveable, always abounding in the work of the Lord, forasmuch as we know that our labour is not in vain in the Lord.

Our Father which art in heaven, etc.

Now the God of peace, that brought again from the dead, etc.

II.

Almighty and Ever-blessed God, from this open grave we lift up our hearts unto Thee. We bless Thee that from the midst of death and sorrow we can look to Thee as our Refuge and Strength, and know that Thou carest for us.

We give Thee thanks on behalf of all those who have lived in Thy holy faith and fear and now rest with Thee. We thank Thee for this finished life, for all Thy goodness to our brother (sister) departed, and that Thou hast released him (her) from the pain and weakness of this mortal body. Blessed be Thy name for the assurance Thou hast given us regarding them who fall asleep in Jesus that they have entered on a fuller life beyond. May our life be so hid with Christ in God, that when Christ who is our life shall appear, we also may appear with Him in Glory.

O Thou who art the God of all comfort, who healest the broken in heart and bindest up their wounds, mercifully look on those who are at this time bereaved. Be near to them in their sorrow and let their sorrow draw them nearer to Thee, and consecrate them for Thy service. Let Thy grace enable them to say, not my will but Thine be done, and in them let patience have her perfect work. May their minds be stayed on Thee, and be filled with Thy peace.

Grant, O God, unto every one of us that as we know neither the day nor the hour when the Son of Man cometh, we may live as those who wait for their Master, having our lamps burning and our loins girt. May we be enabled to persevere and abound in every good work and word, that sanctified by the Spirit, we may have an entrance ministered to us abundantly into the everlasting kingdom of our Lord and Saviour to whom in the name of the Father and the Holy Spirit be glory for ever.

Now we commit dust to dust, ashes to ashes, earth to earth, looking to Jesus who shall change these bodies of humiliation and make them like unto His own glorious Body, according to the power that worketh in us.

Our Father who art in Heaven, etc.

The grace of our Lord Jesus Christ, the love of God the Father and the fellowship of the Holy Spirit be with us all for ever. Amen.

Section IV.

ORDINATION AND INDUCTION OF A MINISTER.

I.—Preparatory.

On the day fixed for the Ordination, the Presbytery meets in the session house or hall of the Church where the service is to take place, some time before the hour of public worship, and is constituted in the usual way. The minister appointed to preach and preside at the Ordination is Moderator *pro tempore*, if he does not hold that position in the Presbytery in ordinary course. It is strongly recommended (1) that at least two ministers should take part in the service—the one to "preach and ordain," the other, who should be a man of some ministerial experience, to address minister and people after the Ordination; (2) that sermon and addresses should be short, so that due time may be given for praise and prayer, and that the whole service may be concluded within a reasonable space. This ought to be matter of arrangement beforehand between the ministers appointed to conduct the service.

It is customary that ministers from a distance, and those representing sister Churches in the parish or district, should be "associated with the Presbytery," and should join with them in the laying on of hands.

The service of praise should have special consideration. Such psalms and hymns as the following may be used in the first part of the service :—

Ps. lxv. 1-4—"Praise waits for Thee in Zion, Lord."
  „ lxviii. 7-11—"O God, what time Thou didst go forth."
  „ lxviii. 18-20—"Thou hast, O Lord, most glorious."
  „ lxxxiv. 1-7—"How lovely is Thy dwelling-place."
  „ lxxxix. 1-5—"God's mercies will I ever sing."
  „ lxxxix. 15-18—"O greatly blessed the people are."
  „ xcv. 1-6—"O come, let us sing to the Lord."
  „ c.—"All people that on earth do dwell."
  „ cii., 2nd version, 13-22—"Thou shalt arise, and mercy yet."
  „ cvi. 1-5—"Give praise and thanks unto the Lord."
  „ cxv. 12-18—"The Lord of us hath mindful been."
  „ cxxii. 1-5—"I joyed when to the house of God."
  „ cxlvii. 1-5—"Praise ye the Lord; for it is good."
Paraph. 20—"How glorious Zion's courts appear."
Hymn—"The Church's one foundation."
  „ —"Jesus, where'er Thy people meet."
  „ —"We pray Thee, Jesus, who didst first."
  „ —"Pour out Thy spirit from above."
  „ —"Jesus, with Thy Church abide."

SEC. IV.] *ORDINATION OF A MINISTER.* 187

Hymn—" O Jesus, Lord of heavenly grace."
  „ —" I love Thy kingdom, Lord."
  „ —" As with gladness men of old."
  „ —" Pleasant are Thy courts above."
  „ —" The God of Abraham praise."
  „ —" Holy, holy, holy, Lord God Almighty."
  „ —" God reveals His Presence."
Scripture Sentence or Anthem—" God is a spirit."
  „   „   „ —" Holy, holy, holy."
  „   „   „ —" He shall feed His flock."
  „   „   „ —" They that be wise shall shine."
  „   „   „ —" Pray for the peace of Jerusalem."

See also the psalms, hymns, &c., suggested below in connection with the different points in the Ordination service proper.

Such passages of Scripture may be read as Exod. iii. 1-15 ; iv. 1-16 ; xxxiii. 12-19 ; xxxiv. 5-9 ; Josh. i. 1-9 ; Ps. xvi. ; xxv. 1-14 ; xxvii. ; cxix. 1-16 ; cxix. 89-104 ; Isaiah vi. ; xl. 1-11, 26-31 ; lv. ; lxi. ; Jer. i. 4-19 ; Ezek. iii. 1-21 ; xxxiii. 1-9 ; xxxiv. ; Matt. ix. 35-38 ; x. 1-8 ; xxiv. 42-51 ; xxv. 14-30 ; xxviii. 18-20 ; Luke ix. 57-62 ; x. 1-11 ; xii. 35-48 ; John x. 1-18 ; xxi. 15-22 ; Acts i. 1-11 ; ii. 1-21 ; xx. 17-38 ; Rom. i. 1-17 ; Eph. iv. 1-16 ; Col. i. 9-29 ; 1 Tim. iii. ; iv. 6-16 ; vi. 11-21 ; 2 Tim. ii. ; iii. ; iv. 1-8 ; Titus i. ; Heb. xiii. 5-21 ; 1 Peter v. 1-11 ; Rev. i. ; ii. ; iii. ; vii. 9-17 ; xxii. The sermon or lecture should refer to some part of the teaching of Scripture regarding Christ and the Church—the Church's mission, privileges, and work in the world ; the work of the Holy Spirit in the Church ; the nature and duties of the Christian ministry; its difficulties and encouragements; the mutual relations of minister and people, &c. Such passages as those noted above may prove suggestive of suitable texts.

An Ordination service is one of the occasions on which special attention should be given to the Apostolic canons for the worship and meetings of the Church: "Let all things be done unto edification," and "Let all things be done in seemly form, and according to order" (1 Cor. xiv. 26, 40). It is fitting and seemly, *e.g.*, that all the ministerial members of Presbytery should wear gown and bands, as on the Lord's Day. They ought to come into the Church together in an orderly way, following the Moderator from the session house. They should sit together, along with the Presbytery elders, beside or in front of the pulpit or communion table, so that the whole action may be *visibly* a Presbyterial one. Care and thought should be given beforehand to all the minor arrangements for good order in the Church in connection with the different parts of the service—including even such details as the provision of pen and ink for signing the formula at the proper time. This implies, of course, some consultation beforehand on the part of the officiating ministers, the Presbytery clerk and Presbytery officer, with the interim Moderator of Session, the Session Clerk, and the Church officer of the congregation concerned.

II.—OUTLINE OF ORDINATION SERVICE.

1. Narrative of steps taken by the Presbytery.
2. Questions put and Formula signed.
3. Prayer (brief) for grace to keep vows taken, and pause for silent prayer.

SEC. IV.] ORDINATION OF A MINISTER. 189

4. Hymn of the Holy Spirit ("Veni Creator Spiritus" or other).

5. Ordination prayer, and laying on of hands of the Presbytery.

6. Admission to Pastoral Charge, and right hand of fellowship given

7. Praise (Doxology, Scripture Sentence, Psalm, or Hymn).

[8. Repetition of the "Apostles' creed."]

9. Charge to newly-ordained Minister and to Congregation.

10. Prayer.

11. Praise.

12. Benediction.

13. Minister welcomed by his people at door of Church.

14. Close of Meeting of Presbytery.

III.—Notes on above Order of Service.

After the sermon and singing of a verse or two of a psalm or hymn (see list for selection given above).

1. *A brief narrative of proceedings of Presbytery in the case*, prepared by its clerk, is read from the pulpit by the Moderator, ending with words to this effect: "All these things having been done according to the law and usage of the Church, the Presbytery are now prepared to ordain the said Mr A. B. to the office of the holy ministry, and to admit him to the pastoral charge of this congregation (or, in the case of a minister who has been already ordained, "to induct the said Mr A. B. to the pastoral charge of this congregation"), as soon as he shall have given satisfactory answers to the following questions,

appointed by the Church to be put to all who are ordained to the ministry, or admitted to any charge."

2. *Questions put and Formula signed.*[1]

The minister-elect stands up, and the Moderator puts the appointed questions to him from the pulpit. He signifies his assent by bowing, or by audible response. The Moderator then adds: "You will at this point sign the Formula, which contains the substance of the questions now answered." After this has been done, it is fitting that, with the approval of the Presbytery, the question given in Appendix I. should be put to the Congregation and answered by them, so as to bring out *their* side of the mutual covenant entered into by pastor and people, and publicly to confirm the promises already made by them in the call addressed to their minister.[2]

---

[1] See Appendix I. for questions to probationers before Ordination and to ministers before Induction, with additional question for the congregation, and with the formula to be signed

[2] This is in accordance with the "Form and Order of the Election of the Superintendent, which may serve in Election of all other ministers," as given in the Service book referred to in the First Book of Discipline (1560) as "The Book of our Common Order." This Election and Ordination Service was in general use in the Church of Scotland for fully sixty years after the Reformation. It was first used "at Edinburgh, the 9th day of March 1560, John Knox being Moderator," in connection with the appointment of Mr John Spottiswood to be Superintendent of Lothian. Several questions were put to the congregation and answered by them. *Inter alia:* "They were asked 'If they would have the said Mr John as Superintendent? If they would honour and obey him as Christ's minister, and comfort and assist him in everything pertaining to his charge?' They answered: 'We will; and we do promise him such obedience as it becometh the sheep to give unto their pastor, so long as he remaineth faithful in his office.'" *Knox's Works* (Laing's ed.) ii. 145; Book of Common Order (Sprott and

3. *Prayer for grace to keep the vows taken.*

After the answers both of the minister-elect and of the people have been received, there may suitably follow a short collect or sentence of prayer by the presiding minister, such as is given in Appendix II., and an opportunity for a few moments of silent prayer on the part of the Congregation[1] for their minister, for themselves, and for the cause of Christ in the special circumstances of their parish and neighbourhood. With a view to this, the Moderator, after the brief petition offered by himself, shall say: "let us now lift up our hearts in silent prayer to God for His servant and people here, and for His cause in this place."

4. *Hymn of the Holy Spirit.*

A hymn, such as the "Veni Creator Spiritus" ("Come, Holy Ghost, our souls inspire"), or "Our blest Redeemer, ere He breathed," may well come in here. Both in praise and prayer there should be very special reference to the Holy Spirit in every Ordination Service. During the singing of this hymn the Moderator leaves the pulpit and takes his place in the centre of the Presbytery. The minister-elect kneels in front of him. The other Members of Pres-

---

Leishman's ed.), pp. 19, 22. Questions of this sort are answered by the congregation at the Ordination and Induction of Ministers in the American Presbyterian Churches, and in the United Presbyterian Church of Scotland. Comp. "Form of Service for the Ordination of a Bishop and his Installation at the same time as Pastor of a Church," in *General Liturgy.* New York and Chicago, 1883, p. 77. This service book, drawn up by Prof. Hopkins, of Auburn Theol. Seminary is on strictly Presbyterian lines.

[1] So in the Ordination Service of the Church of England, and in the Order for Ordination of a minister in the "Euchologion" of the Scottish Church Service Society, 5th ed., p. 248.

bytery and Ministers associated with them stand along with the Moderator, the whole Congregation kneeling at the words, " Let us pray."

5. *Ordination Prayer and laying on of the hands of the Presbytery.*

The Ordination Prayer may be on the lines of those given in Appendix II. The essential points to be kept in view are (1) Ordination to the Office of the Ministry in the Church of Christ is always to be distinguished from admission to the exercise to that office in a particular sphere. There ought, therefore, to be in the prayer, first of all, a solemn setting apart to office in the name of Christ and by the authority of the Church, and thereafter prayer for blessing on the Minister ordained in the Pastoral Charge into which he is now inducted. (2) There should be special prayer that the Holy Spirit may be given to the brother now ordained to fit him for all the work of the Ministry, both in the particular sphere on which he is this day entering, and wherever his lot may be cast hereafter. Such petitions for the special gifts and guidance of the Holy Spirit come in with impressive effect in the Ordination Service of 1560, referred to above,—which was no doubt drawn up by John Knox, —in the Ordination Prayer, in " the Benediction," and in " The last Exhortation to the Elected."[1]

6. *Admission to Pastoral Charge; right hand of fellowship given.*

The Ordination Prayer being ended, and the Minister ordained having risen, the Moderator shall say : " In the name of the Lord Jesus Christ, the only King and Head

[1] See Appendix II.

of the Church, and by the authority of this Presbytery, I declare you to be ordained to the office of the Holy Ministry; I receive and admit you to the Pastoral Charge of this Congregation and to a seat in this Presbytery, with all the rights and privileges belonging thereto: And in token thereof I now give you the right hand of fellowship."

The Moderator then gives his hand to the newly-ordained minister, and is followed in this by the other Members of the Presbytery.

In the case of a Minister already ordained, who is now simply to be inducted into the Pastoral Charge of the Congregation, the necessary changes and omissions in prayer are slight, and can be easily made. The clause "I declare you to be ordained to the office of the Holy Ministry," is of course omitted; and there is no repetition of the laying on of hands.

7. *Praise after the Ordination and Admission.*

The following may serve for selection:—

Ps. cvi. 48—"Blessed be Jehovah, Israel's God."
 ,, cxvi. 17-19—"Thank offerings I to Thee will give."
 ,, cxxi.—"I to the hills will lift mine eyes."
Sentence—"The Lord bless thee and keep thee."
 ,, —"Cast thy burden on the Lord."
 ,, —"Now unto Him that is able."
Hymn—"Praise God, from whom all blessings flow."
 ,, —"Glory be to God the Father."
 ,, —"Praise ye the Father, God the Lord, who gave us."
 ,, —"O praise the Father, praise the Son."

8. *The Apostles' Creed.*

After the singing at this point, which should be brief, there may very suitably come in, where circumstances allow of its being done to edification, a repetition of the "Apostles' Creed" by Minister and Congregation and Members of Presbytery together, as expressing their common faith. This is in accordance with John Knox's "Order of the Election of Elders and Deacons in the Kirk of Edinburgh," which was approved by the General Assembly of 1582 (Sess. 12), and ordered to be of use in the whole Church in the Ordination and Admission of Elders.[1] In this interesting little form of service, after the Ordination Prayer, which ends with the Lord's Prayer, there follows "*the rehearsal of the Belief.* After the quhilk shall be sung this portion of the 103rd psalm, verse 19 ('The heavens high are made the seat') to the end of that psalm. After the quhilk shall this short admonition be given to the elected: 'Magnify God, who hath of His mercy called you to rule within His Kirk,'" &c., ending with prayer.—Knox's *Works*, ii. 154.

9. *Charges to the newly ordained Minister and the Congregation.*

These are delivered from the pulpit, the minister appointed for this part of the Service having taken his place there during the preceding singing. The minister addressed should stand, the address being reasonably short.

---

[1] "Book of the Universal Kirk of Scotland" (ed. Peterkin), p. 250. Andrew Melville was Moderator of this Assembly.

10. *Concluding Prayer.*

This may be on the lines of what is given in Appendix II.

11. *Praise.*

Such Psalms and Hymns as the following are suitable :—

Ps. xxiii.—" The Lord's my Shepherd : I'll not want."
,, lxxii. 17-19—" His name for ever shall endure."
,, cxxii. 6-9—" Pray that Jerusalem may have."
,, cxxxii. 13-18—" For God of Zion hath made choice."
,, cxxxiv.—" Behold, bless ye the Lord, all ye."
,, cxxxvi., First or Second Version, 1-4, 23-26—" Give thanks to God, for good is He."
Paraph. ii.—" O God of Bethel by whose hand."
,, lxv. 5-9, 11—" Hark how the adoring hosts above."
,, lxvii. 12—" O may we stand before the Lamb."
Hymn—" Jerusalem the golden."
,, —" Onward, Christian soldiers."
,, —" Now thank we all our God."
Doxology—" From all that dwell beneath the skies."
,, —" Now to Him that loved us, gave us."
,, —" Halleluiah ! Halleluiah ! "
,, —" To Father, Son, and Holy Ghost."
,, —" Blessed, blessed be Jehovah."

12. *Benediction.*

Heb. xiii. 20-21—" The God of peace," &c.

Or, " The peace of God, which passeth all understanding, keep your hearts and minds in the knowledge and love of God and of His Son Jesus Christ our Lord ; and the blessing of God Almighty, the Father, the Son, and the Holy Ghost, rest upon you and abide with you for ever." Amen.

13. *Minister welcomed by his people at door of Church.*

While the closing Psalm or Hymn is being sung, the newly-ordained or inducted minister takes his place in the porch or vestibule of the Church, accompanied by two or three of the Presbytery or other friends; and the people, as they retire after the benediction, have an opportunity of shaking hands with him at the door.

14. *Close of Meeting of Presbytery.*

The Presbytery return to the session-house, and conclude their meeting there. The name of the newly-ordained or inducted minister is added to the Roll.

APPENDIX.

I.

I.—QUESTIONS TO BE PUT TO PROBATIONERS BEFORE ORDINATION; AND ALSO TO A MINISTER ALREADY ORDAINED, AT HIS ADMISSION TO A PASTORAL CHARGE.

(1.) Do you believe the Scriptures of the Old and New Testaments to be the Word of God, and the only rule of faith and manners?

(2.) Do you sincerely own and believe the whole doctrine contained in the Confession of Faith, approven by former General Assemblies of this Church, to be founded upon the Word of God; and do you acknowledge the same as the confession of your faith; and will you firmly and constantly adhere thereto, and to the utmost of your power assert, maintain, and defend the same, and the purity of worship as presently practised in this Church?

SEC. IV.] ORDINATION OF A MINISTER. 197

(3.) Do you disown all Popish, Arian, Socinian, Arminian, Erastian, and other doctrines, tenets, and opinions whatsoever, contrary to, and inconsistent with, the foresaid Confession of Faith?

(4.) Are you persuaded that the Presbyterian government and discipline of this Church are founded upon the Word of God, and agreeable thereto; and do you promise to submit to the said government and discipline, and to concur with the same, and not to endeavour, directly or indirectly, the prejudice or subversion thereof, but to the utmost of your power, in your station, to maintain, support, and defend the said discipline and Presbyterian government by Kirk-Sessions, Presbyteries, Provincial Synods, and General Assemblies?

(5.) Do you believe that the Lord Jesus Christ, as King and Head of the Church, has therein appointed a government in the hands of Church-officers, distinct from, and not subordinate in its own province to, civil government, and that the Civil Magistrate does not possess jurisdiction or authoritative control over the regulation of the affairs of Christ's Church; and do you approve of the general principles embodied in the Claim, Declaration, and Protest, adopted by the General Assembly of the Church of Scotland in 1842, and in the Protest of Ministers and Elders, Commissioners from Presbyteries to the General Assembly, read in presence of the Royal Commissioner on 18th May 1843, as declaring the views which are sanctioned by the Word of God, and the standards of this Church, with respect to the spirituality and freedom of the Church of Christ, and her subjection to Him as her only Head and to His Word as her only standard?

(6.) Do you promise to submit yourself willingly and

humbly, in the spirit of meekness, unto the admonitions of the brethren of this Presbytery, and to be subject to them, and all other Presbyteries and superior judicatories of this Church, where God in His providence shall cast your lot; and that, according to your power, you shall maintain the unity and peace of this Church against error and schism, notwithstanding of whatsoever trouble or persecution may arise, and that you shall follow no divisive courses from the doctrine, worship, discipline, and government of this Church?

(7.) Are not zeal for the honour of God, love to Jesus Christ, and desire of saving souls, your great motives and chief inducements to enter into the function of the holy ministry, and not worldly designs and interests?

(8.) Have you used any undue methods, either by yourself or others, in procuring this call?

(9.) Do you engage, in the strength and grace of Jesus Christ, our Lord and Master, to rule well your own family, to live a holy and circumspect life, and faithfully, diligently, and cheerfully to discharge all the parts of the ministerial work, to the edification of the body of Christ?

(10.) Do you accept of and close with the call to be pastor of this congregation, and promise, through grace, to perform all the duties of a faithful minister of the gospel among this people?

II.—FORMULA TO BE SUBSCRIBED BY ALL MINISTERS AND ELDERS AT THE TIME OF THEIR ADMISSION.

I, ... do hereby declare, that I do sincerely own and believe the whole doctrine contained in the Confession of Faith, approven by former General Assemblies of this Church to be the truths of

SEC. IV.] ORDINATION OF A MINISTER. 199

God; and I do own the same as the confession of my faith; as likewise I do own the purity of worship presently authorised and practised in the Free Church of Scotland, and also the Presbyterian government and discipline thereof; which doctrine, worship, and Church Government, I am persuaded, are founded on the Word of God, and agreeable thereto: I also approve of the general principles respecting the jurisdiction of the Church, and her subjection to Christ as her only Head, which are contained in the Claim of Right and in the Protest referred to in the questions already put to me; and I promise that, through the grace of God, I shall firmly and constantly adhere to the same, and to the utmost of my power shall, in my station, assert, maintain, and defend the said doctrine, worship, discipline, and government of this Church, by Kirk-Sessions, Presbyteries, Provincial Synods, and General Assemblies, together with the liberty and exclusive jurisdiction thereof; and that I shall, in my practice, conform myself to the said worship, and submit to the said discipline, government, and exclusive jurisdiction, and not endeavour, directly or indirectly, the prejudice or subversion of the same; and I promise that I shall follow no divisive course from the doctrine, worship, discipline, government, and exclusive jurisdiction of this Church, renouncing all doctrines, tenets, and opinions whatsoever, contrary to, or inconsistent with, the said doctrine, worship, discipline, government, or jurisdiction of the same.

III.—QUESTION TO BE PUT TO THE CONGREGATION AFTER THE QUESTIONS HAVE BEEN ANSWERED AND FORMULA SIGNED BY THE MINISTER-ELECT.

Do you, the Members and Adherents of this Congregation, acknowledge and receive Mr A. B., in accordance with the Call already given to him, to be your Pastor, and the Minister of Jesus Christ unto you? And do you promise to give him all due honour, encouragement, and obedience in the Lord? If so, be pleased to signify this now by rising to your feet.

II.

SPECIMEN FORMS OF PRAYER AT THE ORDINATION OF A MINISTER.

1. *Prayer for grace to keep vows taken.*

After the questions to the minister-elect and to the congregation have been put and answered, the presiding minister may say:

"Almighty God, who hath put into your hearts these good resolutions, enable you severally, as minister and people, to fulfil the same, to the glory of His holy name and the edifying of His Church, through Jesus Christ our Lord. Amen."[1]

2. *Ordination Prayer.*

Almighty God, our Heavenly Father, who for the good of Thine household dost set over them faithful and wise stewards, who shall give them their portion of meat in due season: Bless Thy servant now to be set apart to the ministry of the Word and Sacraments in Thy House.

---

[1] From "Form of Receiving an Elder" in "The Liturgy and other Divine Offices of the Church." London, 1880, p. 424 (slightly altered).

O Lord Jesus Christ, who didst love Thy Church and didst purchase it to Thyself with Thine own blood, and who hast promised to be with Thy people always, even unto the end of the world: Be with us now, we beseech Thee, as in Thy Name, and by the authority of this Presbytery (here the Moderator and other ministers of the Presbytery shall lay their hands on the head of the brother to be ordained), we ordain this Thy servant to the office of the ministry with the laying on of hands. May he be filled with the Holy Ghost and with power. May the blessing of God the Father, the Son, and the Spirit, One God, rest upon him and fit him for all service in the Church.

O God, the Father of Lights, the Giver of every good and perfect gift, make this Thy servant wise to win souls, strong in faith and hope and love—teach him to follow Christ fully. May the joy of the Lord be his strength. May he be among those who turn many unto righteousness, who shall shine as the stars for ever and ever. Make him helpful to his brethren and to all the flock over which he is set this day in the Lord, as a pastor and bishop. And in the end may he hear the Master's voice saying to him:—"Well done, good and faithful servant. Thou hast been faithful over a few things, I will make thee ruler over many things. Enter thou into the joy of thy Lord."

Now unto Him that is able to keep you from falling, and to present you faultless before the presence of His glory with exceeding joy, to the only wise God our Saviour, be glory and majesty, dominion and power, now and ever. Amen.[1]

---

[1] The opening sentence of this prayer is taken, with slight alteration, from the liturgy above referred to, p. 424.

3. *Prayer after Ordination and Admission of Minister.*

Almighty God, who hast from the beginning chosen and called a Church unto Thyself upon the earth, and hast promised by the lips of Thy Son that the gates of hell shall not prevail against it: we thank Thee for Thy goodness to us this day in Thy House. Do Thou continue Thy loving-kindness to this Congregation and to Thy servant who has now been set over them in holy things. Give testimony to the Word of Thy grace among them through him. May the Holy Spirit work mightily and effectually among this people through the ministry of the Gospel. May souls be born again in this place. May the careless be awakened. May sinners be converted unto God, and His own people built up in holiness and comfort and in all Christian service through faith unto salvation. Bless the elders and deacons, those who lead in the service of praise, those who teach the young, those who visit the sick, and all workers for Christ and His Church in this Congregation. Prosper and guide all their work and witness for Christ and for the Gospel in this parish and neighbourhood.

Heavenly Father, with whom is the fulness of the Spirit, we beseech Thee to bless Thy whole Catholic Church in this land and throughout the world. Gather Thy people more into one under Christ the Head. May all bitterness and unkindness, all needless divisions and misunderstandings between Thy true people, be taken away. May grace, and mercy, and peace be multiplied to all who love our Lord Jesus Christ in sincerity. We pray especially for that branch of Thy Church with which we are connected, for all who hold

SEC. IV.] ORDINATION OF A MINISTER. 203

office therein, that they may fulfil their several ministries aright, and for all the members of our Church, that they may be living members in the body of Christ, and may bring forth fruit to His praise.

Pour out Thy Holy Spirit upon all men. Hasten the time when all nations shall be blessed in Christ, and the knowledge of the glory of the Lord shall cover the earth as the waters cover the sea. We ask all for the sake of Him who hath taught us to pray, saying —" Our Father, which art in heaven," etc.

JOHN KNOX'S PRAYERS AT THE ORDINATION OF THE FIRST SUPERINTENDENT OF THE LOTHIANS.[1]

1. *Ordination Prayer.*

"O Lord, to whom all power is given in heaven and on earth, Thou who art the Eternal Son of the Eternal Father, who hast loved Thy Church and given Thyself for it, and hast appointed therein Teachers, Pastors, and Apostles to instruct, comfort, and admonish Thy people: Look upon us mercifully, O Lord, and send unto this our brother, whom, in Thy name, we now charge with the chief care of Thy flock within the bounds of Lothian, such portion of Thy Holy Spirit that he may rightly divide Thy Word among them. Give unto him, good Lord, a mouth and wisdom, whereby the enemies of Thy truth may be put to shame, Thy sheep fed, and the blind and ignorant illuminated with the knowledge of Thy will for their salvation. All this we crave of Thee, and the Father, and the blessed Spirit, as by Thee, our Lord and King, and only Bishop, we are taught

[1] Shortened, and with some slight verbal changes. Comp. Knox's *Works*. (Laing's ed.), ii. 143-150.

to pray, saying — 'Our Father, which art in heaven,' etc.

The prayer ended, the rest of the Ministers and Elders present, in sign of their consent, shall take the elected by the hand, and then the chief minister shall give the Benediction as followeth :—

2. *Benediction.*

God, the Father of our Lord Jesus Christ, who hath commanded His Evangel to be preached to the comfort of His elect, and hath called thee to the office of a watchman over His people; multiply His graces with thee; illuminate thee with His Holy Spirit; comfort and strengthen thee in all virtue; govern and guide thy ministry to the praise of His Holy Name, the furtherance of Christ's Kingdom, and the comfort of His Church; and finally, to the assurance of thine own conscience in the day of the Lord Jesus, to whom, with the Father, and with the Holy Ghost, be all honour and glory, now and ever. Amen.

3. *The last Exhortation to the Elected.*

Take heed to thyself and unto the flock committed to thy charge. Feed the same carefully, not as it were by compulsion, but of very love, which thou bearest to the Lord Jesus. Walk in simplicity and pureness of life, as it becometh the true servant and ambassador of Christ.

Be not discouraged in adversity, but set before thee the example of the prophets, apostles, and the Lord Jesus, who in their ministry endured contradiction, contempt, persecution, and death. Fear not to rebuke sin. If anything succeed prosperously with thee, be not puffed up with pride; but ever let that word of the Apostle remain in thine heart, 'What hast thou which thou hast not received? If thou hast received, why gloriest thou?'

Comfort the afflicted; help the poor; exhort others to mercy and good works. Be not solicitous for things of this life, but be fervent in prayer to God for the increase of His Holy Spirit. And finally, so behave thyself in this holy vocation as that God may be glorified in thy ministry. So shalt thou shortly obtain the victory and receive the crown promised when our Lord Jesus, the Chief Shepherd, shall appear in His glory; whose Almighty Spirit assist thee and us to the end. Amen.

Then sing the 23rd Psalm."

Section V.

ORDINATION AND ADMISSION OF ELDERS AND DEACONS.

I.—Preparatory.

On the Lord's Day appointed for the Ordination, the Elders and Office-bearers elect meet in the Session-house some time before the hour of public worship. The Court having been constituted, and the order of procedure arranged, the Session enter the Church at the hour of service, the brethren about to be ordained seating themselves together in front of the pulpit.

The usual service should be shortened, so as to allow

due time for the ordination. Such passages of Scripture as the following may be read :—Exod. xviii. 13-27; Numb. xi. 16, 17, 24-29; Psalm xxiv.; Isaiah lxii. 6-12; Acts vi. 1-7, xx. 17-32; Rom. xii. 1-18; Eph. iv. 1-16; 1 Tim. i. 1-13, iii.; 1 Peter v. 1-11. Psalms and Hymns should be chosen suitable to the special service of the day. The sermon or lecture should bear on some aspect of the Scripture doctrine of the Church, the nature of Church government, the duties of office-bearers and members, &c. Besides the passages noted above, such texts as the following may prove suggestive :—Acts xiv. 23; 1 Cor. xii. 27, 28; 1 Thess. v. 12; Phil. i. 1; 1 Peter iv. 10.

II.—OUTLINE OF ORDINATION SERVICE.

1. Narrative of steps taken.
2. Questions put [and Formula signed].
3. Ordination Prayer.
4. Admission to office, and right hand of fellowship given.
5. Scripture Sentence, Psalm or Hymn.
6. Charge to office-bearers and people.
7. Prayer.
8. Praise.
9. Benediction.
10. (Formula signed, if not at previous point.) Close of Session.

III.—NOTES ON ABOVE ORDER OF SERVICE.

1. Minister reads from the pulpit a brief narrative of steps taken in the election of Elders and Deacons,[1] naming those who have been chosen by the congrega-

[1] Comp. "Practice of Free Church of Scotland," chap. I, Part II. 3.

SEC. V.] ORDINATION OF ELDERS, ETC.

tion and have agreed to accept office; ending thus: "It is now my duty, in the name and by the authority of the Kirk-Session, to ordain these brethren [naming them] to the office to which they have been chosen, [to induct to office in this congregation the following (naming them), who have been already ordained elsewhere], and to receive them as members of the Kirk-Session [or Deacons' Court] when they have given satisfactory answers to the following Questions appointed by the Church."

2. The office-bearers elect stand up. The Moderator puts to them from the pulpit the Questions appointed.[1] They signify their assent by bowing, or by audible response. There may here suitably follow a Question to the congregation—see Appendix I.—This is done at the Ordination of Elders and Deacons, as well as of Ministers, in the American Presbyterian Churches. It is in accordance with the "Form and Order of the Election of the Superintendent, which may serve in election of all other ministers, at Edinburgh, the 9th day of March, 1560; John Knox being Moderator." See quotation given above in connection with "Order for Ordination of Ministers."—p. 190. The formula which embodies the substance of the Questions put, may be signed at this point in presence of the congregation, as in the Ordination of Ministers. This, if it can be conveniently done, forms an impressive part of the service. If it is thought better to defer it, the signatures should be appended before the Session is closed, after the congregation has been dismissed.[2]

[1] See Appendix I. Questions for Elders and Deacons, with additional Question for the Congregation.

[2] Comp. Act 1874, 2; 1892, 4. In Appendix II., the Declaratory

3. The questions having been duly answered, the Moderator leaves the pulpit and takes his place in front of the office-bearers-elect, who should kneel. The members of Session should stand on either side of the Moderator, to shew that the act of ordination is a Sessional one, in which they all have a share. The Moderator then offers the Ordination prayer. This may be on the lines of the specimen forms of prayer given in Appendix III. pp. 215-219. It ought always to include an express setting apart of the new office-bearers in the name of Christ and by authority of this court of His Church to the office of Elder or Deacon, "commendation of them to the Lord for the work which they are to fulfil," and prayer that the Spirit of God may be specially given to them to make them faithful in duty and serviceable to the Church.

As the Westminster Assembly's Form of Church Government puts it, "Ordination is the solemn setting apart of a person to some public Church office" by those who represent the Church. In all ordinary circumstances, this should be done by those already in office. The laying on of hands is not essential to Ordination, although it is a suitable and Scriptural accompaniment of it. The custom of our Church has generally confined the imposition of hands to the Ordination of Ministers only. But there is no ground in principle for its not taking place also in the case of Elders and Deacons. Where it is judged expedient and for edification, the Moderator, as representing the Session, may lay his hands on the heads of

Act of 1892, and the further statement regarding it in Act ix. of Assembly 1894, are given in full. All office-bearers are entitled to answer the Questions and subscribe the Formula in view of these Acts.

the brethren to be ordained at the point in the Ordination prayer at which they are formally set apart to office. The other elders present may join with them in this action, as is done in the United Presbyterian Church. In the case of office-bearers already ordained, but now to be admitted to the exercise of their office in this particular congregation, there is no repetition of the laying on of hands; but there should be special reference to them in prayer.

4. Prayer being ended, and the office-bearers now ordained having risen, the Moderator shall say: " In the name of the Lord Jesus Christ, the King and Head of the Church, and by the authority of this court in His House, we hereby declare you to be ordained to the office of Elder [or Deacon]; and we admit you to the exercise of that office in this congregation with all rights and privileges belonging thereto. And in token thereof we now give you the right hand of fellowship." The Moderator shall then give his hand to each of the brethren newly ordained (or admitted), and may be followed in doing so by the other Elders present.

5. A Scripture Sentence (such as "The Lord bless you and keep you" &c.), Psalm, or Hymn, may then be sung.

6. The Minister gives from the pulpit, a brief exhortation (1) to the new office-bearers, who may stand, and (2) to the congregation, as to their respective duties and the spirit in which these should be discharged.

7. Prayer (brief).

8. Praise. (*e.g.* Ps. ciii. 19-22; cvi. 1.5; cxxii. 6-9; Hymns: "Pour out Thy Spirit from on high;" "Come, Holy Ghost;" "Ye servants of the Lord.")

9. Benediction.—Heb. xiii. 20, 21; or 2 Cor. xiii. 14.

10. After the congregation has been dismissed, the minister and office-bearers remain in the Church, or return to the Session-house. The newly ordained office-bearers sign the Formula, if this has not been done previously. Any needful arrangements as to districts are considered, if time allows; and the Meeting of Session is closed with prayer.

APPENDIX.

I.

Elders.

Questions to be put before Ordination.[1]

1. Do you believe the Scriptures of the Old and New Testament to be the Word of God, and the only rule of faith and manners?

2. Do you sincerely own and declare the Confession of Faith, approven by former General Assemblies of this Church, to be the confession of your faith; and do you own the doctrine therein contained to be the true doctrine, which you will constantly adhere to?

3. Do you own and acknowledge the Presbyterian Church Government of this Church by Kirk Sessions, Presbyteries, Provincial Synods, and General Assemblies, to be the only Government of this Church; and do you engage to submit thereto, concur therewith, and not to endeavour, directly or indirectly, the prejudice or subversion thereof?

4. Do you believe that the Lord Jesus Christ, as King

---

[1] Practice, ed. 4th, p. 155.

and Head of the Church, has therein appointed a government in the hands of Church officers, distinct from, and not subordinate in its own province to civil government, and that the Civil Magistrate does not possess jurisdiction or authoritative control over the regulation of the affairs of Christ's Church; and do you approve of the general principles embodied in the Claim, Declaration, and Protest, adopted by the General Assembly of the Church of Scotland in 1842, and in the Protest of Ministers and Elders, Commissioners from Presbyteries to the General Assembly, read in presence of the Royal Commissioner on 18th May 1843, as declaring the views which are sanctioned by the Word of God, and the standards of this Church, with respect to the spirituality and freedom of the Church of Christ and her subjection to Him as her only Head, and to His word as her only standard?

5. Do you promise to observe uniformity of worship and of administration of all public ordinances within this Church, as the same are at present performed and allowed?

6. Do you accept the office of an Elder of this Congregation, and promise, through grace, faithfully, diligently, and cheerfully, to discharge all the duties thereof?

[Take in *Question to the Congregation* from next page, unless Deacons are to be ordained at same time, in which case the questions to the latter are to be put after No. 6 of the Questions to Elders. Thereafter the Question to the Congregation and signing of the Formula follow. If the Formula is to be signed before the Congregation, the Minister adds:—" You will at this point sign the Formula, which contains the substance of the questions you have now answered."]

Deacons.

Questions to be put before Ordination.[1]

1. Do you believe the Scriptures of the Old and New Testament to be the Word of God, and the only rule of faith and manners?

2. Do you sincerely own and receive, as in accordance with Holy Scripture, the system of Evangelical Truth taught in this Church, and set forth in the Westminster Shorter Catechism?

3. Do you approve of the Presbyterian government and discipline of this Church; and are you persuaded that the Civil Magistrate has no jurisdiction or authoritative control over the regulation of the affairs of Christ's Church?

4. Do you accept of your call to the office of Deacon in this Congregation, and promise, through grace, faithfully, diligently, and cheerfully, to discharge all the duties thereof?

Question to the Congregation.

Do you, the Members and Adherents of this Congregation, acknowledge and receive these brethren as ruling Elders (or as Deacons); and do you promise to give them all due honour, encouragement, and obedience in the Lord?[2] If so, be pleased to signify this by rising to your feet now.

---

[1] Act I. 1884.

[2] When the ordination is one of Deacons only, the reference to "obedience" shall be omitted, and the clause read, "all due honour and encouragement in the Lord."

II.

1. Declaratory Act anent Confession of Faith—Act xii., 1892 :—

"Whereas it is expedient to remove difficulties and scruples which have been felt by some in reference to the declaration of belief required from persons who receive license or are admitted to office in this Church, the General Assembly, with consent of Presbyteries, declare as follows :—

That, in holding and teaching, according to the Confession, the Divine purpose of grace towards those who are saved, and the execution of that purpose in time, this Church most earnestly proclaims, as standing in the forefront of the revelation of Grace, the love of God—Father, Son, and Holy Spirit—to sinners of mankind, manifested especially in the Father's gift of the Son to be the Saviour of the world, in the coming of the Son to offer Himself a Propitiation for sin, and in the striving of the Holy Spirit with men to bring them to repentance.

That this Church also holds that all who hear the Gospel are warranted and required to believe to the saving of their souls; and that in the case of such as do not believe, but perish in their sins, the issue is due to their own rejection of the Gospel call. That this Church does not teach, and does not regard the Confession as teaching, the fore-ordination of men to death irrespective of their own sin.

That it is the duty of those who believe, and one end of their calling by God, to make known the Gospel to all men everywhere for the obedience of faith. And that while the Gospel is the ordinary means of salvation for those to whom it is made known, yet it does not follow, nor is the Confession to be held as teaching, that any who die in infancy are lost, or that God may not extend His mercy, for Christ's sake, and by His Holy Spirit, to those who are beyond the reach of these means, as it may seem good to Him, according to the riches of His grace.

That, in holding and teaching, according to the Confession of Faith, the corruption of man's whole nature as fallen, this Church also maintains that there remain tokens of his greatness as created in the image of God; that he possesses a knowledge of God and of duty; that he is responsible for compliance with the moral law and with the Gospel; and that, although unable without the aid of the Holy Spirit to return to God, he is yet capable of affections and actions which in themselves are virtuous and praiseworthy.

That this Church disclaims intolerant or persecuting principles, and does not consider her office-bearers, in subscribing the Confession, committed to any principles inconsistent with liberty of conscience and the right of private judgment.

That while diversity of opinion is recognised in this Church on such points in the Confession as do not enter into the substance of the Reformed Faith therein set forth, the Church retains full authority to determine, in any case which may arise, what points fall within this description, and thus to guard against any abuse of this liberty to the detriment of sound doctrine, or to the injury of her unity and peace."

2. Act anent Declaratory Act, 1892, on Confession of Faith—Act ix. 1894:—

"Whereas the Declaratory Act, 1892, was passed to remove difficulties and scruples which had been felt by some in reference to the declaration of belief required from persons who receive licence, or are admitted to office in this Church, the Assembly hereby declare that the statements of doctrine contained in the said Act are not thereby imposed upon any of the Church's office-bearers as part of the Standards of the Church; but that those who are licensed or ordained to office in this Church in answering the questions and subscribing the Formula, are entitled to do so in view of the said Declaratory Act."

III.

Specimen Forms of Prayer at Ordination of Elders and Deacons.

I.

Almighty and everlasting God, the God and Father of our Lord Jesus Christ, we give praise and thanks unto Thee for the fellowship of Thy Church on earth, and for all the offices and ordinances of Thy House. Bless, we beseech Thee, these Thy servants who have been chosen and called by Thy people here to the office of Elders [and Deacons] in Thy Church and in this Congregation. Remember each one of them for good. Supply in them all that they feel to be lacking. Grant all that Thou seest they have need of for this ministry.

And as we now, in the name of the Lord Jesus Christ, and by authority of this Court in His Church [here the minister, as representing the Session, or the minister and elders together, may lay his or their hands on the heads of the office-bearers elect] do ordain these brethren to the office of Elder [and Deacon], we commend them to Thee and to the Word of Thy grace. May the presence of the Great Shepherd and Overseer of souls be with them now and always. May the Holy Spirit dwell in them richly, as a Spirit of power, and love, and a sound mind.

[We commend unto Thee also our brother in the Eldership [Deaconship] who is this day added to our number, beseeching Thee to bless him also abundantly with all needed blessing, and to prosper him in all work for the Lord to which he shall set his hand among us. May he, and all those whom Thou hast sent to take part with us in this ministry in Thy Church, have much encouragement in all their service for the Lord and for His cause.]

2.

Almighty God, who art the only Author of all good things, we bless Thee for the fellowship of Thy Church on earth, and for all its ordinances and means of grace. Especially we render thanks unto Thee at this time that Christ, when He ascended to Thy right hand, received gifts for men, and that He hath given some to be ministers of the Word and some to be overseers and shepherds of the flock, for the perfecting of the saints, for the work of the ministry, for the edifying of the body of Christ.

We thank Thee now for the gift to this Congregation of these Thy servants who have been chosen to take part with us in this ministry, and into whose hearts Thou hast put it to accept the call.

And as we now, in the name of the Lord Jesus Christ, the King and Head of the Church, [here the Minister, or the Minister and Elders together, may lay his or their hands on the heads of the Elders elect] do ordain them to the office of Elder in Thy Church, we commend them to Thee and to the Word of Thy Grace. Grant unto them a double portion of Thy Spirit. May

He fit them for the care and oversight of Thy flock in this place. Make them ensamples to all that believe, in word, in manner of life, in love, in faith, in purity. Teach them how to win souls to Christ, to comfort the afflicted, to support the weak, to restore wanderers, to feed the lambs of the flock. And when the Chief Shepherd shall appear may they receive the crown of glory, which fadeth not away.

Our heavenly Father, we beseech Thee to bestow Thy grace also upon all the members of this congregation, that they may receive these Thy servants with gladness, and submit themselves to them as set over them in the Lord. May they esteem them very highly in love for their work's sake, counting the elders that rule well worthy of double honour, and seeking to be followers of them as they follow Christ. Now unto Him that is able to do exceeding abundantly above all that we ask or think, according to the power that worketh in us, unto Him be glory in the Church by Christ Jesus, throughout all ages, world without end. Amen.

[Partly from Presbyt. Forms of Service. 2nd ed. 147.]

3.

Almighty God our heavenly Father, the giver of all good gifts, who hast appointed in Thy Church, besides Ministers of the Word, rulers and helpers, for its oversight and government, we beseech Thee to bless these Thy servants, chosen by this congregation to serve in its Eldership. And as we now, in the name of Christ and by authority of this Court in His Church, set them apart to the work and office to which they have been called, we pray that all needed gifts and grace may be given them from Thyself. Fill them with Thy Holy

Spirit. Give them favour and influence with the people. Make them diligent and faithful in all things, and wise with that wisdom which cometh from above. May they tend the flock of God in this place, taking the oversight thereof, not by constraint, but willingly, not for worldly advantage, but of a ready mind, according to Thy will. May they in all things be ensamples to the flock; and when the Chief Shepherd shall appear, may they receive the crown of glory that fadeth not away.

[Partly from Dr Vincent's *Minister's Handbook*. New York, 1882.]

4.

For Ordination of Deacons.

Almighty God our heavenly Father, who in Thy Divine Providence hast appointed different offices in Thy Church, and hast given by Thy Spirit diverse gifts to men, fitting them for ministry therein; we beseech Thee to bless these Thy servants now called to the work and office of Deacon.

O Lord Jesus Christ, who, although Thou wert rich yet for our sakes didst become poor that we through Thy poverty might be made rich, do Thou own and ratify what we do in Thy house, as now in Thy name we set apart and consecrate these our brethren to this office. Give them Thine own spirit of sympathy with all human needs and sufferings, and of self-denying service in behalf of all who are in want and affliction.

Holy Spirit of power and love, of counsel and of comfort, guide Thou them in all their ministry of love in the midst of us. Make them to be wise and faithful in all the outward business of God's House entrusted to them. Teach them how to foster the grace of liberality among Thy people here, to watch over the treasury of the Church and to care aright for the poor. So serving well as Deacons, may they gain to themselves a good standing in Thy Church and great boldness in the faith which is in Christ Jesus.

[Partly from Dr A. A. Hodge's Manual of Forms, 1882.]

Section VI.

THE LICENSING OF PROBATIONERS.

I.—Preparation.

After the Presbytery has completed and sustained the trials of students, it is well that a special public service be held for the purpose of licensing the candidates as preachers of the Gospel. This is specially appropriate in towns, and in cases where more than one are to receive license at the same time.

The Presbytery should appoint two or more ministers to conduct the service. These ministers should carefully arrange what parts of the service are to be taken by each. Care should also be taken to prevent the sermon and the addresses from covering the same ground. If it is thought better to have no sermon, then Nos. 5 and 6 in the following Order will be omitted. The presiding minister may take Nos. 1 to 6 and 16 and 17, and the other minister Nos. 7 to 15.

Great attention should be paid to the length of each portion of the service. Without such care, the service is apt to be unduly prolonged.

It will greatly help to secure reverence and decorum, if arrangements are made whereby the Presbytery and the candidates may be conveniently seated, and if a table and chair with pen and ink are provided in a suitable place for the signing of the formula.[1]

II.—Order of Service.

1. Psalm or Hymn.
2. Prayer.
3. Reading of Scripture.
4. Psalm or Hymn.
5. Short Sermon.
6. Hymn.
7. Prayer.
8. Announcement of names of candidates, with brief narrative of procedure.
9. Questions to candidates.
10. Signing the Formula.
11. Declaration of License; right hand of fellowship given.
12. Prayer.
13. Hymn or Anthem.
14. Address (1) to Licentiates.
     (2) to Congregation.
15. Prayer.
16. Hymn.
17. Benediction.

[1] The signing of the Formula before the congregation was made *obligatory* in the case of all "persons inducted into any spiritual office or function in this Church" by Act II., 1874. The obligation was relaxed, as regards all office-bearers except Ministers, by Act IV., 1892. It is *optional* at present, as regards Probationers, Elders, and Deacons, whether the signing should take place in public, immediately after the Questions have been answered, or in private, before the Presbytery or Session, at the close of the service. But it is desirable that it should be in public.

III.—Notes on above Order of Service.

1. Appropriate Psalms and Hymns:—Ps. xlvi. 1-5; lxv. 1-4. Hymns, "Lord God, the Holy Ghost"; "Breathe on me, Breath of God."

3. Appropriate Scripture Lessons are:—Isa. vi.; Isa. lv.; Isa. lxi. 1-6; Acts i. 1-14; Acts ii. 1-21; 2 Cor. v. 11-21; vi. 1-10; 1 Tim. i. 1-17; 2 Tim. ii. 1-15; Rev. i. 4-18.

4. Appropriate Psalms:—Ps. lxi. 4-8; lxvii.

6. Appropriate Hymns:—"The Spirit breathes upon the Word"; "O Word of God incarnate."

7. This prayer should be very brief, consisting of petitions for blessing on the Word preached, and for the Divine Presence in the solemn actions that are to follow.

8. The Candidates should stand up. Their names should be distinctly read by the presiding minister. He should state that the Candidates have duly completed the required course of study, that the Presbytery has satisfied itself both as to their attainments in scholarship, and as to their personal character and their motives in seeking to enter the Ministry, and that, with the sanction of the Provincial Synod, the Presbytery is now to proceed to license them as preachers of the Gospel.

9. When the statutory questions are read the candidates should answer audibly "I do." (The latter part of question 3rd requires the answer "I am.") When there are several candidates they may signify their assent by inclination of the head.[1]

11. When the Moderator formally licenses the

---

[1] See the Questions in Appendix.

candidates, which should be done "in the name of the Lord Jesus Christ as King and Head of the Church and by authority of this Court in His House," all the members of Presbytery should stand up, and thereafter follow the Moderator in shaking hands with the licentiates. The good order and impressiveness of this part of the service will depend much on the previous arrangements as to proper seating.

12. This prayer should include :—Thanksgiving for the Word, and for the institution of preaching; confession of human weakness and imperfection in the solemn work of preaching the Gospel; Petitions in behalf of those now licensed to preach, that they may be filled with the Spirit, that they may grow in grace and in the knowledge of God, and that they may be true ambassadors for Christ, and able ministers of the New Covenant, not of the letter but of the Spirit. Prayer should also be offered for their present guidance in study and in work, and that they may be led in God's own time to suitable spheres of usefulness at home or abroad.

Note.—The helpfulness of this prayer will depend on its relevancy to the special circumstances, and it should be limited to these.

13. Appropriate Psalms and Hymns are :—Psalms xliii. 3-5; cxxxii. 13-18. Hymns, "Pour out Thy Spirit from on high," "Come, Holy Ghost, our souls inspire," "Blow ye the trumpet, blow."

14. The Address to the licentiates may deal with such points as the following :—The nobility and responsibility of the preacher's office; present position of the licentiates that of men putting on their armour not putting it off. Need for continued study. The

SEC. VI.] LICENSING OF PROBATIONERS. 223

supreme importance of personal piety. The value of the experience gained, should some time elapse before settlement in a charge. A minister requires to be an administrator as well as a student. Hence the need for knowledge of men, of affairs, of ecclesiastical procedure, and of church management. The probationers should also be exhorted to look upon their preaching prior to being "called," as the work of Evangelists. They are not to consider their preaching as merely an effort to obtain a charge. In itself it is a distinct and noble work. And they occupy a distinct and important office. By preaching and working in this spirit, they will be delivered from the self-consciousness and straining after outward effect which the system of popular election sometimes produces.

The Address to the congregation, which should be extremely brief, may be an exhortation to prayer for Divinity Students and Professors, for Probationers, for all whose relation to Divine things is endangered by professionalism, and for congregations engaged in choosing pastors, that wisdom and brotherly harmony may be manifested in every step.

15. The concluding prayer should include :—Thanksgiving for the Church and all ordinances of Divine appointment, and for the privileges enjoyed in this land; prayer for blessing on the Church universal, and especially on the Free Church of Scotland and all its work at home and in the mission field, for her Colleges, and for this Presbytery.

16. Appropriate Psalms and Hymns :—Psalms lvii. 17-19; cxxii. 6-9. Hymns, "Jesus shall reign"; "O Spirit of the living God"; "For all the saints"; "Thou whose Almighty Word."

APPENDIX.

QUESTIONS TO BE PUT TO PROBATIONERS BEFORE THEY ARE LICENSED TO PREACH THE GOSPEL.[1]

1. Do you believe the Scriptures of the Old and New Testaments to be the Word of God, and the only rule of faith and manners?

2. Do you sincerely own and believe the whole doctrine of the Confession of Faith, approven by the General Assemblies of this Church, to be the truths of God, contained in the Scriptures of the Old and New Testaments; and do you own the whole doctrine therein contained as the confession of your faith?

3. Do you sincerely own the purity of worship presently authorised and practised in this Church, and also own the Presbyterian government and discipline, and are you persuaded that the said doctrine, worship and discipline and Church government, are founded upon the Holy Scriptures, and agreeable thereto?

4. Do you believe that the Lord Jesus Christ, as King and Head of the Church, has therein appointed a government in the hands of Church-officers, distinct from, and not subordinate in its own province to, civil government, and that the Civil Magistrate does not possess jurisdiction or authoritative control over the regulation of the affairs of Christ's Church; and do you approve of the general principles embodied in the Claim, Declaration, and Protest, adopted by the General Assembly of the Church of Scotland in 1842, and in

---

[1] Act XII., 1846.

the Protest of Ministers and Elders, Commissioners from Presbyteries to the General Assembly, read in presence of the Royal Commissioner on 18th May 1843, as declaring the views which are sanctioned by the Word of God, and the standards of this Church, with respect to the spirituality and freedom of the Church of Christ, and her subjection to Him as her only Head, and to His Word as her only standard?

5. Do you promise that, through the grace of God, you will firmly and constantly adhere to, and in your station, to the utmost of your power, assert, maintain, and defend the said doctrine, worship, and discipline, and the government of this Church by Kirk-Sessions, Presbyteries, Provincial Synods, and General Assemblies?

6. Do you promise that in your practice you will conform yourself to the said worship, and submit yourself to the said discipline and government of this Church, and not endeavour, directly or indirectly, the prejudice or subversion of the same?

7. Do you promise that you shall follow no divisive courses from the doctrine, worship, discipline, and government of this Church?

8. Do you renounce all doctrines, tenets, or opinions whatsoever, contrary to, or inconsistent with, the said doctrine, worship, discipline and government of this Church?

9. Do you promise that you shall subject yourself to the several judicatories of this Church?

The presiding Minister may add: You will at this point sign the Formula, which contains the substance of the Questions you have now answered.

Section VII.

DEDICATION OF A CHURCH.

I.—Preparation.

As the Presbytery authorises the building of a Church, and as the dedication usually takes place on a week day, this service should be attended by the Presbytery in its official capacity; and it is desirable that the various parts of the service should be assigned to different officiating ministers. The suggestions made as to the need of special attention to the apostolic canons in 1 Cor. xiv. 26, 40 at Ordinations and Inductions (see above p. 188) should be considered and applied here also. Particular consideration should be given to the service of praise, so that it may be suited both to the circumstances, and to the capacities of the congregation and its choir. This implies judicious arrangement beforehand between the Minister and the leader of the praise, and with the representatives of the Presbytery or other officiating Ministers. In view of the directions given in the Reformed Liturgies and some recently published Dedication Services, the following order is suggested :—

II.—Order of Dedication Service.

1. Scripture Sentences.
2. Prayer of Invocation.
3. Praise.
4. Prayer.
5. Old Testament Lesson.
6. Prose Chant.

7. New Testament Lesson.
8. Prayer of Intercession and the Lord's Prayer.
9. Praise.
10. [The Apostles' Creed.]
11. Prayer of Dedication.
12. Praise.
13. Sermon.
14. Prayer.
15. Praise.
16. Benediction.

III.—Notes on above Order.

1. A selection of **Scripture Sentences** as at p. 229.

2. **Specimen forms** of **Prayer of Invocation** are given at pp. 231-233.

3. The **Psalms of Praise** most commonly used at the **opening** of a Dedication Service are Psalm xxiv. 7-10—"Ye gates, lift up your heads on high," Psalm lxv. 1-4—"Praise waits for Thee," or Psalm c.—"All people that on earth do dwell."

4. **Prayer of Thanksgiving** for means of grace and confession of shortcoming in the use of them. This prayer should be brief.

5. Suitable passages for an **Old Testament lesson** are 1 Chron. xxix. 1-25, 2 Chron. vi., 1 Kings viii. 22-53.

6. **The Psalms** recommended in the Reformed Liturgies for a Dedication Service are Psalms xlviii., lxxxiv., lxxxvii., cxxxii. The prose version of one of these psalms may be chanted, but where that is not possible, there might be sung such hymns as "The Church's One Foundation," "O Thou whose hand has brought us," "Christ is our corner-stone."

7. **Suitable passages** to be read from the **New Testament** may be found in 1 Cor. iii., Eph. ii., Rev. xxi.

8. **Prayer of Intercession**: concluding with the Lord's Prayer; for the minister, office-bearers, and congregation; for the Church of our fathers, and the unity of the whole Church of Christ; for the coming of Christ's kingdom and the blessing of God on all missions; for the country and its rulers; thanksgiving for the faithful departed, and ascription of praise as in Eph. iii. 20, 21, "Now unto Him that is able," etc. The Congregation may be requested, at this stage in the service, to offer **The Lord's Prayer.**

9. **Praise.** This song of praise should be a Hymn of the Holy Spirit : "Veni, Creator Spiritus," "Our Blessed Redeemer," "Spirit Divine, attend our prayers."

10. The minister may fitly at this point in the service invite the congregation to join with the Church of Christ throughout the world in making confession of their faith in the words of **The Apostles' Creed.**

11. **Prayer of Dedication**—[See Appendix pp. 233-238.] This prayer ought to include :—

(1) Adoration and Thanksgiving, specially for the building of this House of Prayer, for God's goodness in connection with the carrying out of the work (freedom from accidents, etc.).

(2) Dedication of the building to God's service and glory.

(3) Prayer for all who, in days to come, shall worship, and for those who shall minister in holy things.

(4) Petitions—that the sacrifices of praise, confession and supplication, may be according to God's will —that the gospel may be preached with power —that the sacraments may be observed with

reverence, and honoured by Him who appointed them—that this Sanctuary, now dedicated to the worship of God, may be a place of holy memories, and a birthplace of many souls.

(5) The prayer may be concluded with such words as: "Arise, O Lord, into Thy rest, Thou and the ark of Thy strength"—or, "Now unto Him that loved us," etc.

12. "**Te Deum Laudamus**" or the "**Ter Sanctus**" may here be sung, or such Psalms as cvii. 1-9; cxi. 1-5; cxxxiv.; cxlviii. 2nd version; cl.; or such Hymns as "Praise the Lord! Ye heavens adore Him," "Praise ye Jehovah! Praise the Lord most holy," "The God of Abraham praise," "Thou whose unmeasured temple stands."

13. **Sermon.**

14. **Brief Prayer** for blessing on the services of the day.

15. **Concluding psalm or hymn of praise**: Psalms cxxii. 6-9; xc. 14-17; lxxii. 17-19; "O God of Bethel," "Now thank we all our God."

16. **Benediction** as in Hebrews xiii. 20; with Apostolic Benediction, 2 Cor. xiii. 14.

APPENDIX.

I.—Scripture Sentences.

"But will God in very deed dwell with men on the earth? Behold, heaven and the heaven of heavens cannot contain Thee; how much less this house which we have built. Have respect therefore to the prayer of Thy servants and to their supplication, O Lord our God, to hearken unto the cry and the prayer which Thy servants pray before Thee: that Thine eyes may be open upon this house day and night, upon the place whereof Thou hast said that Thou wouldst put Thy name there: to hearken unto the prayer which Thy servants pray in this place: hear Thou from heaven Thy dwelling-place, and when Thou hearest forgive."

2 Chron. vi. 18-21.

"Thus saith the high and lofty One that inhabiteth Eternity, whose name is Holy: I dwell in the high and holy place, with Him also that is of a contrite and humble spirit, to revive the spirit of the humble, and to revive the heart of the contrite ones."

Isaiah lvii. 15.

"Behold the tabernacle of God is with men, and He will dwell with them, and they shall be His people, and God Himself shall be with them, and be their God."

Rev. xxi. 3.

"Except the Lord build the house they labour in vain that build it: except the Lord watch the city the watchman waketh but in vain."

Psalm cxxvii. 1.

"The Lord hath chosen Zion: He hath desired it for His habitation. This is my rest for ever, here will I dwell for I have desired it. Arise, O Lord, into Thy rest, Thou and the ark of Thy strength. Let Thy priests be clothed with righteousness, and let Thy saints shout aloud for joy."

Psalm cxxxii. 14.

"Praise waiteth for Thee, O God, in Sion: and unto Thee shall the vow be performed. O Thou that hearest prayer, unto Thee shall all flesh come. Iniquities prevail against me: as for our transgressions, Thou shalt purge them away. Blessed is the man whom Thou choosest, and causest to approach unto Thee, that he may dwell in Thy courts: we shall be satisfied with the goodness of Thy house, even of Thy holy temple."

PSALM lxv. 1-4.

"How amiable are thy tabernacles, O Lord God of hosts; our soul longeth, yea, even fainteth for the courts of the Lord, our heart and our flesh crieth out for the living God."

PSALM lxxxiv. 1, 2.

"One thing have we desired of the Lord, that will we seek after: that we may dwell in the house of the Lord all the days of our life, to behold the beauty of the Lord and to inquire in His temple."

PSALM xxvii. 4.

"O send out Thy light and Thy truth: let them lead us, let them bring us to Thy holy hill, even to Thy tabernacles: then will we go unto the altar of God, to God our exceeding joy."

PSALM xliii. 3.

II.—PRAYERS OF INVOCATION.

I.

(1) Almighty and most merciful God, without whose grace no man can serve Thee acceptably, be pleased now to pour out upon us Thy Holy Spirit as a spirit of

grace and supplications, that we may seek Thee with a true heart and right spirit, worthily magnify Thy Holy Name, and rejoice in Thy salvation, through Jesus Christ our Lord. Amen.

(2) Most gracious God, who art ever more ready to hear us than we are to pray unto Thee, and hast promised that Thy tabernacle shall be with men, fill this house, we beseech Thee, with Thy presence, inspire and direct the worship that shall here be offered unto Thee, hear and answer the prayers which from this place shall ascend to Thy Throne, for the sake of Him whom Thou hearest always, our only Advocate and Mediator, Jesus Christ our Lord. Amen.

II.

(1) Almighty and ever blessed God our Heavenly Father, we beseech Thee, as we are now assembled for the first time within this House which has been built for Thy worship, to fulfil unto us the word of promise on which Thou hast caused us to hope, that Thine eyes may be open toward this House day and night, even toward the place of which Thou hast said My Name shall be there. In this service of dedication, as in all worship that shall be offered to Thee here in days to come, give us grace to seek the advancement of Thy glory, the good of our fellowmen, and the salvation of our own souls. We ask it through Jesus Christ our Lord. Amen.

(2) O Lord Jesus Christ, who didst vouchsafe Thy presence at the feast of the dedication of the Temple, be present, we beseech Thee, at the dedication of this

Sanctuary, and, as Thou hast given Thy people the assurance that where two or three are gathered together in Thy Name, Thou art in the midst of them, grant we pray Thee that Thy promise may be fulfilled to us who are assembled here to-day, and Thine shall be the praise and the glory for ever. Amen.

(3) Most blessed and Holy Spirit of all grace, without whose aid nothing is strong and nothing holy, who alone by Thy presence canst hallow any place, grant, we beseech Thee, that the souls of all true worshippers in this house may be consecrated by Thine indwelling, Who art the promise of the Father, by Jesus Christ our Lord. Amen.

"Glory be to the Father," etc.

III.—DEDICATION PRAYER.

Almighty and ever-blessed God our Heavenly Father, Who didst fulfil Thy Word unto our fathers, hear now the prayer of their children, and as we give thanks to Thee that in Thy Providence this house has been built for Thy worship, be pleased, we beseech Thee, to accept now our dedication of it to Thy praise. We thank Thee for all the tokens of Thy Fatherly care and love which are around us this day, that the workmen have been kept from harm and disaster while the work went on, and that their skill and labour have been crowned by Thee with good success. Who are we that we should be able to make this offering, for all things are of Thee and of Thine own have we given Thee? But accept, we beseech Thee, the work of our hands, and bless this House in every part of it, that the very doorposts of the Sanctuary may be consecrated to

Thy glory. Preserve in quietness and in the fear of Thy Holy Temple, Thy children who shall come hither in future days. May those who shall minister in holy things be men after Thine own heart, clothed with power and with the beauty of the Lord our God. When Thy children come to make mention of the loving kindness of the Lord in the House of the Lord, do Thou so fill their souls with thanksgiving that they may sing Thy praise with melody in their hearts. Do Thou, whose ear is ever open to the cry of the penitent, listen to every sincere confession of sin, and answer every prayer for pardon that may be offered by Thy children, that Thy peace may visit the troubled spirit and heal the wounded conscience. When they lift up their hearts and voices in supplication, hear Thou, in heaven Thy dwelling-place, and when Thou hearest, forgive: and though they may often know not what to ask, do unto them, we beseech Thee, exceeding abundantly above all that they can ask or think. Let Thy consolations meet the afflicted here, and may the mourner be comforted.

May the Word of the Truth of the Gospel, read and preached from this place, be ever the quick and powerful sword of the Spirit, the word also of comfort unto him that is weary and of light to every darkened soul. Honour the administration of the Sacraments in this Church, according to Thy promise and according to our hope. May little children who are dedicated to Thee in holy baptism grow up in Christ, and when the Lord's Table is spread from time to time, may the Master meet with His disciples, to cheer their hearts, and may He be known of them in the breaking of the bread. Let this House be a true birthplace of souls, a place of holy memories, a Sanctuary of fellowship with Thee our Father and with Jesus Christ Thy Son. Listen, we beseech Thee, to the voice of this our prayer. Let Thy work appear unto Thy servants, and Thy glory unto their children: and let the beauty of the Lord our God be upon us: yea, the work of our hands establish Thou it.

Now unto Him that loved us, and washed us from our sins in His own blood, and hath made us kings and priests unto God and His Father: to Him be glory and dominion for ever and ever. Amen.

Another Dedication Prayer.

(*From Directory for Public Worship, prepared by Committee of Synod of Presbyterian Church of England in* 1892.)

After 9 or 10, the people still standing, the Minister shall say: Beloved Brethren, this House which has been built for the honour and service of Almighty God, we now solemnly dedicate unto the Father, the Son, and the Holy Ghost, one living and true God; to Whom be glory and majesty, dominion and power, for ever and ever. Amen.

Let us pray: O God our Father, most High, most Holy, unto whom we have access by one Spirit through our Lord Jesus Christ, we praise Thee, we bless Thee, we give thanks unto Thy name for Thy loving-kindness and Thy truth. We humbly beseech Thee now to accept our dedication of this House which we have built for Thy service, and to grant that within its walls Thy people may worship Thee in spirit and in truth from generation to generation.

At what time soever Thy servants hold their solemn assemblies in this place, may it please Thee so to inspire them with Thy Holy Spirit, that the words of their lips and the meditations of their hearts may be acceptable in Thy sight—receive their sacrifice of praise—when the penitent pour out their hearts before Thee, hear Thou in heaven Thy dwelling-place, and when Thou hearest, forgive.

Grant, we entreat Thee, that the true doctrine of Thy gospel may be taught in this place, and the Sacraments of Thy grace duly administered, that they who are athirst may draw water with joy out of the wells of salvation. May Thy Word work effectually here in the hearts of them that believe, so that they may grow in the grace and knowledge of our Lord Jesus Christ, being strengthened unto every good work and word. May those who were dead in sins be made alive here unto Thee, and such as have gone astray be brought back unto the Shepherd and Bishop of their souls. Satisfy Thy servants with the goodness of Thy house, that young men and maidens, old men and children, may praise and magnify Thy holy name.

And unto Him that is able to do exceeding abundantly above all that we ask or think, according to the power that worketh in us, unto Him be glory in the Church, by Christ Jesus, throughout all ages, world without end. Amen.

For Prayer at Laying the Foundation or Memorial Stone of a Church, the following may be found suggestive.[1]

Almighty and everlasting God, by whom of old the foundations of the earth were laid : we beseech Thee to

---

[1] It is the Prayer offered by Principal Dykes, at the laying of the Memorial Stone of Westminster College, Cambridge, on 25th May 1897.

SEC. VII.] DEDICATION OF A CHURCH. 237

prosper this work of our hands, which we have undertaken for the upbuilding of Thy kingdom and the glory of Thy holy name. Be pleased to guard the workmen employed upon this building from harm to life or limb; and grant that their labour, being neither marred through negligence, nor interrupted by any disaster, may find through Thy goodness a successful issue.

Lord Jesus Christ, who art the only Head of Thy Church and the Saviour of our souls, may it please Thee to accept the offerings of Thy servants, and to fulfil the counsels of their hearts; so that this House, of which we lay the foundations now, may stand for generations a home of consecrated learning, and a training ground for godly and able Ministers of Thy Gospel. Here let the spirit of concord dwell, the spirit of knowledge and of the fear of the Lord. May they who teach here, and they who learn, alike be taught from Thy lively oracles those mysteries of Divine truth, whereby men are made wise unto salvation.

Most gracious God, the Father of our Lord Jesus Christ, we give Thee thanks for the indwelling of Thy Holy Spirit in Thy universal Church. We entreat Thee to favour with Thy continual benediction all colleges of learning, especially those of this ancient University. And upon all bishops and pastors of Thy flock, with all who at home or abroad declare Thy Word, be pleased to pour down the healthful influence of Thy grace.

O God, who art the blessed and the only Potentate, by whom kings rule: we ask Thee to bless Thy servant our sovereign lady Queen Victoria. Bless Albert Edward, Prince of Wales, the Princess of Wales, and all the Royal House. Grant wisdom to the Queen's Ministers, and to all who are set in places of authority, especially the Mayor and Magistrates of this town. Be pleased to protect the Army and Navy of this kingdom. Prosper its arts and sciences, its commerce and agriculture. Through every rank and calling among our people may peace and temperance, justice and piety prevail to all generations.

These things we humbly ask of Thy Divine goodness through the merits and mediation of Thy Son, our Lord Jesus Christ; unto whom, with Thee and the Holy Ghost, one God, be laud and honour, world without end. Amen.

PRINTED BY
TURNBULL AND SPEARS.
EDINBURGH

www.ingramcontent.com/pod-product-compliance
Lightning Source LLC
Chambersburg PA
CBHW021403230426
43666CB00006B/621